# THE PROBLEM OF HISTORY
## IN MARK
### And Other Marcan Studies

# THE PROBLEM OF HISTORY
# IN MARK
## And Other Marcan Studies

JAMES M. ROBINSON

FORTRESS PRESS                    PHILADELPHIA

First Fortress Press Edition 1982

Library of Congress Cataloging in Publication Data

Robinson, James McConkey, 1924–
    The problem of history in Mark and other Marcan studies.

        Bibliography: p.
        Includes indexes.
        1. Bible. N.T. Mark—Criticism, interpretation, etc.—Addresses, essays, lectures. 2. Gnosticism—Addresses, essays, lectures. I. Title.
    BS2585.2.R6     226'.3067     81-70594
    ISBN 0-8006-1628-6     AACR2

9406K81   Printed in the United States of America   1-1628

# CONTENTS

Introduction                                                                    7

PART ONE: The Messianic Secret and the Gospel Genre

    I   On the *Gattung* of Mark (and John)                              11

   II  Gnosticism and the New Testament                                 40

PART TWO: The Problem of History in Mark

  III  The Problem of History in the Interpretation of Mark            55

  IV  The Marcan Introduction: 1.1–13                                  69

   V  The Exorcism Narratives                                          81

  VI  From the Debates to the Resurrection                             91

 VII  History Since A.D. 30 in Mark                                    102

VIII  Historical Attitude and Communal History                           116

Indexes                                                                       135

# INTRODUCTION

If William Wrede's discovery of the so-called Messianic secret as the center of Marcan theology was at first sensed in the English-speaking world not only as wrong but even as wrong-headed, this may at least in part be due to the fact that Wrede did not succeed in placing his basically valid insight into a meaningful historical context. Therefore, Albert Schweitzer thought he could equally well transfer it even back into the life of Jesus itself. The progressive recognition in our day that Schweitzer's position was in both senses of the word a step backward does not make the presentation by Wrede any more satisfactory. It only makes it all the more urgent that some adequate matrix for the "Messianic secret" be worked out by the ongoing scholarly enterprise, if Marcan theology is to be placed intelligibly in the course of primitive Christian thinking. It is to this end that the first essays in the collection are primarily devoted: "On the *Gattung* of Mark (and John)" and "Gnosticism and the New Testament."[1]

The experiencing of Easter as the decisive turning point in the course of human events could all too easily relegate the life of Jesus itself to no more than a penultimate factor in primitive Christianity. Faith in the vindication of Jesus could have the paradoxical effect of playing down traditions about Jesus by according priority instead to developing the Easter kerygma. The status of the Jesus traditions would in effect be that of the culmination of the Old Testament and John the Baptist, the highest

[1]"On the *Gattung* of Mark (and John)" is a paper commissioned in the spring of 1970 by the Pittsburgh Festival on the Gospels to present the standard scholarly view of Marcan priority over the other canonical Gospels. It was published in *Jesus and Man's Hope*, ed. David G. Buttrick and John M. Bald (A Perspective Book; Pittsburgh: Pittsburgh Theological Seminary, 1970), vol. I, pp. 99–129. "Gnosticism and the New Testament" was commissioned for inclusion in *Gnosis: Festschrift für Hans Jonas*, ed. Barbara Aland (Göttingen: Vandenhoeck und Ruprecht, 1978), pp. 125–43. Since that survey treated other aspects of the New Testament as well, only those parts having to do with Mark, the bulk of the essay (pp. 132–143), are included here. These two essays have been somewhat revised so as to make more explicit their critical front against Wrede and hence their revised understanding of the point of departure for the Marcan composition. This has rendered superfluous the inclusion here of a paper presented at the Journées bibliques of Leuven in August 1971, in which the basic argument of these essays was summarized: "The Literary Composition of Mark," *L'Evangile selon Marc: Tradition et rédaction*, ed. M. Sabbe (Bibliotheca Ephemeridum Theologicarum Lovaniensium 34; Gembloux: Duculot and Leuven University Press, 1974), pp. 11–19.

level prior to the Easter revelation. Traditions about Jesus might at best then function as the text for which an authoritative, inspired kerygmatic interpretation was necessary. But, even so, continuing Easter experiences, either as revelations in themselves or as interpretations of the traditions of Jesus, would relativize and render potentially dispensable those traditions themselves. Such a potentiality could readily receive momentum from a gnosticizing devaluation of the bodily existence that characterized the traditions of Jesus but that, from a gnostic point of view, the resurrected Christ had put aside as an impediment and at best a camouflage of his heavenly glory.

Over against such a trajectory Mark replaces the authoritative role of Easter appearances with Jesus' direct presentation of higher Christian truth to the Church's precursors on his way from Galilee to the cross. The lower level of traditions about Jesus still needing higher interpretation is confined to a first phase of his ministry leading up to Peter's confession at Caesarea Philippi. There the shift is identified with the first prediction of the passion. The Gospel of John in its own way carried through a remarkably similar corrective of the gnosticizing trajectory. Hence, this line of investigation can bring to fruition an insight hardly more than postulated a generation ago: "The secrecy theory is the hermeneutical presupposition of the genre Gospel."[2]

Meanwhile the traditions about Easter were undergoing a similarly motivated corrective, in that their real bodiliness became increasingly prominent, no doubt at the expense of their glorious appearance. The blinding light of the Damascus road gave way to a resurrected Christ who resembled a gardener, a tourist on the way to Emmaus, or a fisherman by the sea, and whose mode of existence was still bodily in that he could eat, be touched, and resume life on earth. With the gnosticizing proclivity of the ongoing Easter traditions thus for the time blunted, Easter stories that affirm the ultimacy of bodily existence could be introduced at the conclusion of the other Gospels.

Advocates of the gnosticizing trajectory could even appropriate the Easter traditions at this more bodily stage of their development. For one could relegate such bodily appearances to a transitional phase in the progressive exaltation of Christ, to be followed by his ascension and then his

---

[2]Hans Conzelmann, "Gegenwart und Zukunft in der synoptischen Tradition," *ZThK* 54 (1957):295; "Present and Future in the Synoptic Tradition," *God and Christ: Existence and Providence (Journal for Theology and the Church* 5), p. 45.

normative disembodied appearances, in which he communicates direct gnostic truth. To be sure Luke already countered such a potential rebuttal by making the emphatically bodily appearances the end of all resurrection appearances. The ascension does not lead to appearances from heaven, except for the Pauline tradition, which Luke plays down as hardly more than a conversion story. Rather there follows in Lucan theology the gift of the Spirit at Pentecost, a form of divine presence that would not be interpreted at the expense of the ultimacy of the traditions about Jesus or his bodily appearances. Thus the higher level that Mark had tacitly denied to the resurrection appearances, but claimed for the period from Caesarea Philippi to the crucifixion could be extended forward to include resurrection appearances as well as backward to embrace all Jesus traditions. Thus the morphology of the Gospel genre becomes intelligible as progressive stages in the trajectory from Easter to orthodoxy.

The other major segment in the present volume comprises *The Problem of History in Mark*.[3] If Luke and John could launch the time of the Church as a distinctive period by the gift of the Spirit at Pentecost or a resurrection appearance, Mark could with the descent of the Spirit on Jesus at baptism launch the kind of eschatological struggle he saw as the meaning of Jesus' history. The way in which Mark brings together various traditions to settle upon this as the beginning of the story is analyzed in the chapter on "The Marcan Introduction: 1.1–13," a topic of investigation continued in section A.A, "The Beginning Point of the *Gattung* Gospel," in the essay "On the *Gattung* of Mark (and John)." Once Jesus' history is launched in this way, the traditions about Jesus as exorcist and miracle worker, though still located in the phase of veiled parabolic teaching, can be given exemplary significance, as is their continuation in the debates with Jewish authorities and disciples. This becomes even more obvious in the chapter on "History Since A.D. 30 in Mark." For there seems to be no basic change

---

[3]*The Problem of History in Mark* (Studies in Biblical Theology 21; London and Naperville: SCM Press and Alec R. Allenson, 1957), fourth impression by Lewis Reprints Ltd. in 1971. This is a compressed version of a dissertation written under Otto A. Piper in the summer of 1954 for a doctorate awarded by Princeton Theological Seminary the following year. The full text of chapters 2—5 was translated into German by Karlfried Fröhlich and published as *Das Geschichtsverständnis des Markus-Evangeliums* (Abhandlungen zur Theologie des Alten und Neuen Testaments, ed. Walter Eichrodt and Oscar Cullmann (Zürich: Zwingli-Verlag, 1956). A critique prepared for a seminar of W. D. Davies by William H. Harter, "The Historical Method in Mark," was published in the *Union Seminary Quarterly Review* 20 (1964):21–38, to which I was invited to respond, "The Problem of History in Mark, Reconsidered," *USQR* 20 (1965):131–147.

in the understanding of history as one moves from Jesus to the Church.
In the introduction to a selection of essays on Mark the editor Rudolf
Pesch points to this chapter's "clear contacts with the approach of redaction
criticism" as illustrative of Willi Marxsen's comment that at the time he
launched redaction criticism in 1956 it was "in the air."[4]

[4]"Geschichte seit dem Jahr 30 n. Chr. im Markus-Evangelium," *Das Markus-Evangelium*,
ed. Rudolf Pesch (Wege der Forschung 411; Darmstadt: Wissenschaftliche Buchgesellschaft,
1979), pp. 113–140. The quotation from Pesch's "Einführung" is from p. 8. He there
quotes from Willi Marxsen, *Der Evangelist Markus. Studien zur Redaktionsgeschichte des Evangeliums* (Göttingen: Vandenhoeck und Ruprecht, 1956, second edition 1959), p. 5.

# PART ONE

# The Messianic Secret and the Gospel Genre

# I

# ON THE *GATTUNG* OF MARK
# (AND JOHN)

### A. *REDAKTIONSGESCHICHTE* AND *GATTUNGSGESCHICHTE*

*Redaktionsgeschichte* has tended to become the focus of research in the Gospels in the period since Willi Marxsen introduced the term in 1956.[1] "Editorial history" would probably be a more fully Anglicized translation of this term than is the current literalistic translation "redaction history." For whereas in German *"Redaktion"* is a more common term than is *"Edition,"* the reverse is true in English.[2] Furthermore, the German language has the ability, for which there is no adequate English equivalent, to run on a series of nouns connected with an "s," making each in effect an adjective modifying the succeeding noun (or an adverb modifying the succeeding adjective). Since in English the Latinizing solution has become quaint (for example, "religio-historical school" for *"religionsgeschichtliche Schule"*), the alternatives are either to unpack the compound German term into a chain of adjectival phrases in reverse sequence (for example, *"Traditionsgeschichte"* as "history of [the transmission of] tradition[s]"), or to retain the German sequence if an adjective is available to substitute for the German substantive, as would be the case if one were to translate *Redaktionsgeschichte* as "editorial history." To be sure, the first wooden translations of such terms are often intentionally literalistic, since the exact intent of the new German formulation is not fully grasped. But once launched, they tend to catch on as *termini technici* in English, and hence to survive due to their function of symbolizing, without further discussion, the school of thought intended. Yet this policy makes the position esoteric,

---

[1]Willi Marxsen, *Der Evangelist Markus: Studien zur Redaktionsgeschichte des Evangeliums*, FRLANT 67 (1956). ET by Roy A. Harrisville, *Mark the Evangelist* (1969).

[2]Martin Dibelius, *Die Formgeschichte des Evangeliums*, 2nd ed. (1933), p. 2 refers to *"Redaktoren,"* but the ET by Bertram Lee Woolf, *From Tradition to Gospel*, p. 3, rightly translates "editors."

and, in such half-translated English dress, gives more the impression of an in-group's school jargon than is intended by the German original.

Ernst Haenchen questioned whether *Redaktionsgeschichte* conveys adequately what Marxsen intended, and himself preferred the designation *Kompositionsgeschichte*.[3] Actually both terms, editing and composition, were already used by the form critics with reference specifically to Mark.[4]

Marxsen's point in introducing the term *Redaktionsgeschichte* as a new category was to argue that form criticism focused attention on the oral smaller units, and that one should now shift attention to the larger written wholes, with a concomitant observation that the Evangelists were more "authors" than the form critics had conceded. The form critics had emphasized that the Gospels did not come from the academic or learned sphere, but from popular traditions handed down from generation to generation, such as the German Faust literature (without benefit of Goethe). "Such a writer of a folk book does not so much have the personality of an author as he is a mere collector, and hence an exponent of a tradition carried on by the people. . . . A synopsis of the various Faust books makes clear that all their writers were only quite secondarily authors, but were in the main collectors, transmitters, and editors, and that the units brought together by them had already previously attained their formal unity."[5]

Actually, when one observes the assessment of Mark by the form critics, on the background of such a classification, one can only be surprised at

[3]Ernst Haenchen, *Der Weg Jesu: Eine Erklärung des Markus-Evangeliums und der kanonischen Parallelen* (1966), p. 24. Marxsen, *Der Evangelist Markus*, p. 7 (ET, p. 15), begins by expressing the view that the editor should be "conceded a special share in the composition of his work."

[4]For example, Rudolf Bultmann, *Die Geschichte der synoptischen Tradition*, 2nd ed. (1931), pp. 362ff., ET by John Marsh, *The History of the Synoptic Tradition*, revised edition 1968, pp. 337ff., has a section entitled "The Editing of the Narrative Material and the Composition of the Gospels," in which section he presents his analysis of the Gospel of Mark (pp. 362–76, ET, pp. 338–51). Martin Dibelius, *Formgeschichte*, p. 2 (ET, p. 3) describes the activity of an editor as "transmitting, grouping, and working over."

[5]Karl Ludwig Schmidt, "Die Stellung der Evangelien in der allgemeinen Literaturgeschichte," EUCHARISTERION (*Gunkel-Festschrift*), FRLANT 36, Part 2 (1923), pp. 95f., 98. This is in effect a paraphrase of formulations from Martin Dibelius, *Formgeschichte*, p. 2 (ET, p. 3). When Marxsen, *Der Evangelist Markus*, p. 7 (ET, p. 15), expresses surprise that Dibelius says that one should *begin* one's understanding of the Gospels with this insight, he overlooks the validity of a form critical classification as the first scholarly objective, itself to be of course based upon interpretation, but then to be presupposed (and of course modified and adjusted as needed) in the detailed exposition of the text.

the extent to which they recognize a theological will at work in the composition of Mark. To be sure, they presupposed Wrede's Messianic secret, and for that reason were more modern than their contemporaries outside of Germany. But one need only compare their own analyses of Mark with those in the subsequent period of *Redaktionsgeschichte* to recognize that, even though their main interest was focused on the oral period, their analyses of Mark are at least as competent as those of their successors.[6]

This current emphasis on the Evangelists as "authors" is somewhat obscured by the term *Redaktionsgeschichte*, since it focuses attention upon the Evangelists precisely as editors rather than authors.[7] Whether the term "composition" is a basic improvement on "redaction" or "editing" can be answered variously, in the light of which nuance of the term "composition" is envisaged. The meaning intended is that the Evangelist does not work mechanically as he compiles and assembles, but works toward a total composition reflecting his theological conception. Put conversely, this means that the method to be worked out would consist in making use of form criticism's identification of the individual units of tradition as the building blocks available to the Evangelist, so as to detect the Evangelist's tendency or theology by observing the way he employs his construction materials to compose a whole, to produce a structure, a Gospel. That is to say, a shift from the designation *Redaktionsgeschichte* to the term *Kompositionsgeschichte* would actually point toward a shift in method. Rather than deriving an Evangelist's theology primarily from the observation of the consistently tendentious way in which he edits a written source available to us for control, one would observe the way he assembles discernible building blocks into a meaningful structure whose form reflects his tendency or theology. That is to say, *Redaktionsgeschichte* would modulate via *Kompositionsgeschichte* into *Gattungsgeschichte*.

In the case of Mark, this modulation in terminology and method from *Redaktionsgeschichte* to *Gattungsgeschichte* does have a distinct advantage over *Redaktionsgeschichte* in the narrower sense (though Marxsen in fact introduced this term with Mark in view). For *Redaktionsgeschichte* has not been

---

[6]Cf., for example, Martin Dibelius, *From Tradition to Gospel*, Ch. VIII, "Synthesis" (in the German edition entitled "Sammlung," that is, "Collection"), and Bultmann in the section cited above.

[7]Marxsen, *Der Evangelist Markus*, p. 11, note 1 (ET, p. 21, n. 17) recognizes this problem, but justifies his terminology by saying he does not want, in designating his "method," to prejudice the conclusion (namely, that the Evangelists were more than just editors, and were in fact theologians and authors).

as fruitful in the case of Mark as in the case of Matthew (Bornkamm) and Luke (Conzelmann), since in the latter two cases we have before us one of their written sources (Mark). Thus their theology can be rather clearly determined by observing their editing activity and disengaging its theological tendency (although for a careful assessment of their theologies, the theoretical question of the relative significance of accepted tradition and tendentious editing needs further elucidation).

In a generation in which the Synoptic problem has been largely dormant, the success of *Redaktionsgeschichte* in clarifying theologies of Matthew and Luke on the assumption of dependence on Mark is perhaps the most important new argument for Marcan priority, just as perhaps the main ingredient lacking in William R. Farmer's argument[8] for Marcan dependence on the other written Gospels is a convincing *Redaktionsgeschichte* of Mark based on that assumption. The very absence of written surviving Marcan sources is perhaps the main reason *Redaktionsgeschichte* has not been as effective with regard to Mark as it has proven to be with regard to Matthew and Luke.

Of course, even on the assumption of Marcan priority one can to some extent reconstruct the pre-Marcan oral units, and thus identify Mark's editorial activity directed toward the oral sources. But the preredactional status of oral sources is always of necessity more conjectural than is that of surviving written sources, even if there may be some fluidity as to just what Marcan text was used by Matthew and Luke; and an editor would probably be more inclined to recast oral traditions freely to suit his needs (as indeed oral transmission would tend constantly to be updating them), whereas he would tend to be relatively more conservative with a written source (just as the fixity of the written source would as time went on widen the theological gap between source and editor). The result is that the editorial hand is much less discernible in the case of oral sources than in the case of surviving written sources. Hence in this age of *Redaktionsgeschichte* the absence of surviving written sources of Mark has tended to leave Mark in obscurity. Much the same is the case with the Fourth Gospel. The trend over the last generation to regard it as basically independent of the Synoptic Gospels had tended to put it methodologically in the same position with regard to written sources as is Mark on the basis of Marcan priority.

[8]*The Synoptic Problem: A Critical Analysis* (1964).

The hope I expressed some years ago,[9] that progress in disengaging an independent written source for John would serve both to put into profile Johannine theology and, by implication, to provide a working hypothesis for the further investigation of Mark, has only to some extent been realized in the intervening years. The recent detailed studies of a Miracles Source used by John have tended to confirm its existence, though not reaching agreement as to its extent (beyond the obvious instances such as the first two miracles, which can be reconstructed from John 2:1–12 and 4:46–54.)[10] But the postulate of a comparable "aretalogy" in the case of Mark is less fully worked out.

The English translation of Dibelius's work inserts a definition of "aretalogy" absent from the German original (but presumably included in the "collaboration" between author and translator to which reference is made on the back of the title page): "the description of the miraculous deeds of the god."[11] This seems to fit the meaning of the rather rare Greek term itself, for example, Sirach 36:14: "Fill Zion with thy 'aretalogies'"; RSV: "Fill Zion with 'the celebration of (thy) wondrous deeds.'" Though the need to supply a definition in the English translation of Dibelius's work indicates the term is less common in English than in German, Dibelius's meaning would nonetheless seem to fit the dominant English usage. *Webster's Third New International Dictionary* defines an aretalogy as "a narrative of the miraculous deeds of a god or hero." This is an accurate definition of the *Gattung* here under consideration. This "standard English" meaning of the term is to be clearly distinguished from another use of the term aretalogy, to refer to "lists of divine claims, prerogatives, and titles," such

---

[9]"The Problem of History in Mark, Reconsidered," *Union Seminary Quarterly Review* 20 (1965): 136f.; "Kerygma and History in the New Testament," *The Bible in Modern Scholarship,* ed. J. Philip Hyatt (1965), pp. 135ff., reprinted in *Trajectories through Early Christianity* by James M. Robinson and Helmut Koester, 1971, pp. 51ff.

[10]Cf. my paper at the organizational meeting of the Gospels Seminar of the Society of Biblical Literature in Berkeley, Dec. 1968, published as "The Johannine Trajectory" in *Trajectories through Early Christianity,* pp. 232–68. That paper analyzes two investigations of the Johannine source, Robert Tomson Fortna's *The Gospel of Signs: A Reconstruction of the Chief Narrative Source Underlying the Fourth Gospel,* SNTS Monograph Series 11 (1970), and Ernst Haenchen's *Das Johannesevangelium* (1980—it was previously available in part in manuscript) and argues that, though diverging in method and results, they confirm the existence of a written miracles source used by John. This problem was discussed in the 1969 session of the Seminar in Toronto. See subsequently W. Nicol, *The Sēmeia in the Fourth Gospel,* Supplements to *Novum Testamentum* 32 (1972); Jürgen Becker, *Das Evangelium des Johannes,* Ökumenischer Taschenbuch-Kommentar, 4 (1979, 1981).

[11]*From Tradition to Gospel,* p. 96.

as the Isis "aretalogies."[12] Although a collection of miracle stories is obviously a *Gattung* quite distinct from a listing of divine titles and distinctions, still a connection in terms of the deity's *aretē* or *virtus* is evident, with the first definition of "aretalogy" nearer the Liddell-Scott translation of *aretē* as "glorious deeds, wonders, miracles," and the second definition nearer the translation, "distinction, fame." In the present context, "aretalogy" refers only to the *Gattung* consisting of a narrative of the miraculous deeds of a god or hero.

If such a correlation in terms of aretalogies could be established between the literary genesis of Mark and John, this would contribute to the solution of the question of how the *Gattung* Gospel could emerge relatively independently in the two documents. For, in view of the plurality of kerygmatic trends in primitive Christianity, and their history-of-religion parallels, the view that one distinctive *Gattung* Gospel emerged sui generis from the uniqueness of Christianity seems hardly tenable. That thesis of form criticism[13] has some relative justification over against the apologists' classification of Gospels as memoirs or histories, and the subsequent exploitation of that initial error to support the possibility of the quest of the historical Jesus on the basis of the Gospels as "historical documents." Yet the correlation of that form critical view to the Barthian transcendent interpretation of Overbeck's *Urgeschichte* did not encourage a search among *Kleinliteratur*, with which the Gospels were conceded to be most kin, for an actual parallel *Gattung* to which attention should be drawn. Dibelius did recognize the individual aretalogy as a "Greek analogy" to individual miracle stories in the Gospels,[14] but did not extend this analogy to larger units or chains of miracle stories emerging as written aretalogies or collections of miracle stories.

Although some miracles are narrated in "paradigms," the miraculous event is not the point of such units; rather it is the *"Novelle,"* the "tale," which revels in the miracle as such. Therefore, if the tendency of the individual unit can be conjectured to have been carried over to the collection, it should be among the *Novellen* that an aretalogy as a collection of miracle stories would be located. Dibelius classifies all the Johannine mir-

---

[12]Cf, for example, the collection in *Hellenistic Religions: The Age of Syncretism*, ed. by Frederick C. Grant (1953), from which the latter definition is quoted, p. 130.

[13]Cf. Karl Ludwig Schmidt, "Die Stellung der Evangelien in der allgemeinen Literaturgeschichte," EUCHARISTERION, Part 2, pp. 50–134.

[14]*From Tradition to Gospel*, p. 154.

acle stories as *Novellen* (2:1ff.; 4:46ff.; 5:1ff.; 6:1ff.; 9:1ff.; 11:1ff.), and thus Fortna's "Signs Source" is in fact a collection of *Novellen*—although Fortna proceeded to extend it to include the passion and resurrection story (with 21:1–14 already one of the "signs"). Mark, on the other hand, contains the miraculous both among paradigms (for example, 1:23ff.; 2:1ff.; 3:1ff.) and among *Novellen:* 1:40–45; 4:35–41; 5:1–20, 21–43, 6:35–44, 45–52; 7:32–37; 8:22–26; 9:14–29. In the section characterized by *Novellen,* H.-W. Kuhn, like the form critics themselves, has postulated a collection of miracle stories imbedded in Mark 4:35—6:51, though compelling reasons for such a theory have not been presented.[15]

There is an interesting and perhaps significant peculiarity in the section of Mark dominated by *Novellen,* namely a doublet, which is made all the more interesting by two additional traits: it recurs in John, and it consists of more than a single episode, indeed seems to be a cycle of *Novellen,* a transition stage between the individual *Novelle* and the written aretalogy. The doublet or triplet is most obvious in terms of the miraculous feeding (Mark 6:35ff.; 8:1ff.; John 6:5ff.). The three cycles do not include identical materials (quite apart from the fact that verbal identity is too rare to encourage the view of one being literarily dependent on the other, or on a common written source). But there is sufficient common material among all three (the crossing of the Sea of Galilee—to different destinations—following the feeding; a subsequent discussion—different in each case—about bread; and so forth), and sufficient material common to various pairs among the three (walking on the water in Mark 6:45–52 and John 6:16–21; similar healings in Mark 6:53–56 and Mark 8:22–26; and so forth), that one is inclined to suspect three variants of a still fluid tradition involving a cycle of miracle stories. The fact that the Johannine discourse on bread is not appended directly to the feeding but is separated from it by the walking on the water suggests that the two miracle stories had already merged so solidly prior to John that he considered them as a single unit. The extent to which omissions, additions, and transpositions may have obscured further parallels than those in the present texts, and the extent to which similarities have been introduced, for example, by Marcan traits entering the two Marcan accounts, or Mark introducing traits from

---

[15]Heinz-Wolfgang Kuhn, *Ältere Sammlungen im Markusevangelium,* SUNT 8 (1971), pp. 191–213. See the criticism by Dietrich-Alex Koch, *Die Bedeutung der Wundererzählungen für die Christologie des Markusevangeliums* (1975), p. 38.

one into the other, continue to be unclear, preventing any certainty as to the existence of such a cycle.[16]

It is this Marcan doublet that leads up to the Caesarea Philippi confrontation. (Luke omits all the material between the first feeding of the multitude and Caesarea Philippi.) Thus the purely formal and rather empty definition of Mark by Martin Kähler as a passion narrative with extended introduction can be brought into sharper profile by describing it from its center outward: The confrontation of Caesarea Philippi seems to be the Gordian knot that must be resolved if we are to understand the Marcan composition.[17] And the drastic operations evident here seem to serve the function of forcing into some kind of ecumenical working relationship two ancient cycles, the passion narrative on the one hand and the *Novellen* cycle and/or aretalogy on the other. Yet the very existence of both these cycles is in question,[18] and thus their use as a basis for Marcan *Redaktionsgeschichte* in a way comparable to the use of Q for Matthew and Luke or of the Miracles Source for John. There are, however, a few instances in Mark comparable to those in John of editing a text so fixed that it may well have been written—the collection of parables in Mark 4 and individual miracles.[19]

B.  *RELIGIONSGESCHICHTE* AND *GATTUNGSGESCHICHTE*

Already the allusion to aretalogies suggests that the question of the emergence of the *Gattung* Gospel cannot be answered without reference to the history of religions. The Fourth Gospel has been quite consistently interpreted in terms of the history of religions; but this has not been the case with the Gospel of Mark to so great an extent. It is the purpose of the present section to illustrate further the suggestiveness of studying Mark and John together, by reference to one segment of the history of religions that has been frequently correlated to John, but has only rarely been considered with regard to Mark: Gnosticism. This is not because

---

[16]See the reservations expressed by Koch, *Die Bedeutung der Wundererzählungen für die Christologie des Markusevangeliums*, p. 38. Yet he does concede that the sequence of the feeding and the crossing of the sea had established itself in the oral tradition.

[17]Cf. the evaluation by Norman Perrin, *Rediscovering the Teaching of Jesus* (1967), pp. 15ff.

[18]With regard to the passion narrative see *The Passion in Mark: Studies on Mark 14—16,* ed. Werner H. Kelber (1976).

[19]For detailed studies of Mark 4:1–34 as containing a pre-Marcan collection of parables see Kuhn, *Ältere Sammlungen im Markusevangelium,* pp. 99–146, and Heikki Räisänen, *Die Parabeltheorie im Markusevangelium,* Schriften der Finnischen Exegetischen Gesellschaft, 26 (1973).

Gnosticism is assumed to be more relevant than other comparisons, but primarily because it is necessary, when new source material emerges, to work it through the whole New Testament and see where it can prove to be of assistance.

It is also worthy of note that such an inquiry was already envisaged by William Wrede in his epochal *Das Messiasgeheimnis in den Evangelien* (1901). First of all, it was Wrede who reversed the then current trend toward separating Mark and John from each other, not only as earliest from latest (where Wrede would agree), but especially as most historical from least historical. By defining Mark as built upon dogmatic theses, Wrede broke down the basic material distinction between Mark and John. Furthermore, he made observations of relevance to the study of the problem of the emergence of the *Gattung* Gospel in two relatively independent documents, by pointing out that specific ingredients of the so-called Messianic secret are less well preserved in Matthew and Luke than in Mark, but recur in striking analogies in John. If Conzelmann is right that "the secrecy theory is the hermeneutical presupposition of the *Gattung* Gospel,"[20] then the prominence of that theory in Mark and John, in contrast to Matthew and Luke (in spite of their having Mark before them), could aid in identifying the ingredients making it possible for the same *Gattung* to emerge at two relatively independent places. For Wrede associated Mark and John in the following terms:

> The view of the literary nature of the Gospel of Mark, which in various respects I have placed over against the common critical treatment of the document, corresponds to some extent to the view which scholarly criticism, that is, free criticism, itself follows in the case of another document—the Gospel of John. This is worth emphasizing, since it points out that there are here no unbridgeable clefts for critical exegetical method, and since one can learn of Mark from the Gospel of John. . . . Of course I have no intention of obscuring the distinction between it and John. It is certainly very great. . . . Nevertheless, the affinity in principle is after all much greater than one generally realizes, precisely because Mark too is already very far removed from the real life of Jesus and is dominated by dogmatically structured concepts. If one looks at Mark with a powerful magnifying glass, one has something like the kind of literary activity that John exemplifies.[21]

---

[20]*ZThK* 54 (1957): 295. ET in *God and Christ: Existence and Providence (Journal for Theology and the Church* 5), p. 45.

[21]*Messiasgeheimnis*, pp. 143–145 (ET, pp. 143–145). Quotations are my own translation.

The Problem of History in Mark

## A. The End Point of the Gattung Gospel

It is obvious that Jesus' resurrection or exaltation meant for primitive Christianity a basic shift from the situation prior to Easter. Early Christological formulas such as Rom. 1:3–4; Phil. 2:6–11; Acts 2:36 reflect a change in Jesus' status, and the gift of the Spirit at this time (Acts 2:33; John 20:22) indicates a comparable change in the disciples' status. The location of the latter two references at the conclusion of two of the Gospels, together with the comparable conclusion of Matthew (28:18–20), in which Jesus' new status of authority is correlated with the disciples' new status as missionaries, suggests that this basic awareness of primitive Christianity could, differently developed, become constitutive for the *terminus a quo* of the gnostic Gospels.

There must have been intermediary stages and interactions between Easter itself and the ultimate outcome, a mutually exclusive polarization of its interpretation with regard to the *Gattung* Gospel. That is to say, in the first generation or so, prior to this polarization, there must have been, side by side, aspects leading not only toward the *Gattung* locating the Gospel prior to and climaxing in Easter, but also aspects pointing toward the *Gattung* placing the Gospel from Easter on. Hence it is legitimate to look for the beginnings of the trajectory leading to the gnostic Gospel *Gattung* within the formative ingredients behind the canonical Gospels, and vice versa. It was Wrede who, with a clairvoyance that is remarkable in view of the inaccessibility to him of the supporting documentation now emerging from Nag Hammadi, sensed this to be the case with regard to Mark and John.

Wrede argued as follows:[22] John 12:16 reports that the disciples did not understand an OT prophecy to refer to Jesus until after he was glorified. Since the prophecy did not deal with the resurrection, this delayed-action interpretation cannot be explained as simply clarification *ex eventu*, but points to a more basic assumption: The earthly ministry of Jesus became clear only with Easter, or, in this case more specifically, the earthly ministry received its *interpretatio biblica* and the OT its *interpretatio christiana* only from Easter on. The same seems implied at 20:9, even though here it is a question of the OT prophesying specifically the resurrection. Similarly, 2:22 dates the *interpretatio christiana* of a saying of Jesus from Easter on, apparently on the basis of the same assumption, even though here too

---

[22]*Messiasgeheimnis*, pp. 182–185 (ET, pp. 184–186).

the saying is specifically a prediction of Easter. When in 13:28 none of the disciples understands Jesus' call upon Judas to do soon what he had to do, the assumption latent in this verse is that with the resurrection they did understand. In 13:7, when Peter does not understand the footwashing, Jesus remarks that though he does not understand it now, he will later—presumably after Easter.

In Mark 9:9f., the disciples are enjoined not to tell of the transfiguration "until the son of man has risen from the dead," a saying the disciples "retain," pondering "what rising from the dead is." (In 9:32 also the disciples do not understand the prediction of the passion and resurrection.) The concept that the story of the transfiguration is to be suppressed until a given point of time, the resurrection, together with the concept that the resurrection is incomprehensible, suggests to Wrede the thesis: "To be sure Jesus does not *make* of this suffering and resurrection a secret for his disciples, yet it *does* remain a secret to them. Afterwards—this is the tacit assumption—that is, of course, from the resurrection on, the scales fall from their eyes."[23] The reproach, "Do you not yet understand?" (8:17,21), is taken not in terms of a progressive revelation to or training of the twelve, but rather as presupposing the permanent lack of understanding of the disciples, their hardness of heart (6:52), for which there is no cure short of basic divine intervention, that is, Easter.

Wrede argued for the necessity of a temporal component just beneath the surface, if the Marcan messianic secret is to make sense at all:

> If then Jesus' revelations remain veiled to the disciples because of their lack of understanding, and indeed to the intimate circle just as much as to the rest, this surely cannot mean that they have no meaning for them at all. Rather Mark must mean that (the revelations) nonetheless actually do come into the possession of the disciples. They become theirs, so to speak materialistically, and carry on with them a sort of latent existence, until the time comes when the blinds are taken from the disciples' eyes, i.e. until the resurrection. In this moment then Jesus' whole self-presentation becomes belatedly effective. What was not understood becomes knowledge now, and now the knowledge is and must be spread abroad. Thus, in spite of all their blindness, the disciples receive from Jesus himself the equipment that they of necessity must have to be his witnesses, his apostles. For this quality of theirs rests on what they received from him himself, received by the transmission of tradition.

---

[23]*Messiasgeheimnis*, p. 95 (ET, p. 95).

*The Problem of History in Mark*

As best I can see, Mark has not actually expressed these ideas in his Gospel. But he can have had no other view. The preferential treatment of the disciples over the crowd, the esoteric instruction imparted to them, surely cannot have been something without purpose and effect. And that it would have been, if one did not constantly look beyond the period of blindness. A few times the idea does indeed after all shimmer through recognizably. In the parable section the motif of lack of understanding recedes, apart from 4:13; for example, the disciples receive the interpretation of the parables, and the direct injunction is given to reveal at some time what is now secret (4:21f.). Also the "retention" of the not-understood saying about resurrection (9:10) seemed to indicate that the intimates, in spite of all momentary incapacity, do take up into themselves the most precious possession.[24]

Hence, Wrede summarizes his analysis of Mark as follows:

We find in Mark two ideas:
1. Jesus keeps his messiahship secret as long as he is on earth.
2. To be sure, he reveals himself to the disciples, in contrast to the crowd, but even for them he remains, in his revelations, for the time being incomprehensible.

Behind both ideas, which often flow one into the other, there lies the shared view that the real knowledge of what he is begins first with his resurrection.[25]

He summarizes the parallel between Mark and John as follows:

Common to both authors is in any case the idea that for the disciples the resurrection separates two times, the time of blindness and that of full knowledge.

Further, in John too Jesus keeps his teaching in a certain sense in hiding, or he communicates it in a way that hinders the hearers from grasping it. To be sure, this is no longer the view of the secret Messiah in Mark's sense, the Messiah who conceals himself. On the contrary, in my opinion this has disappeared, just as the Johannine Christ expressly, from the very beginning, comes forward with the claim to be God's son. Rather what one finds here is to be traced back to the influence that the special concept of Jesus talking in parables has exercised. For this admittedly continues to work clearly and powerfully in John, and it is irrelevant in this connection that the word *paroimia* is only seldom used.[26]

---

[24]*Messiasgeheimnis*, p. 112–113 (ET, pp. 112–113).
[25]*Messiasgeheimnis*, p. 114 (ET, pp. 113–114).
[26]*Messiasgeheimnis*, p. 204 (ET, p. 205).

This suggests that, to the extent one is speaking of a phenomenon broader than Mark (and to a considerable extent even within Mark), the term "messianic secret" is inadequate, focusing attention not on the center of the matter but on one of its various passing manifestations. The whole course of the trajectory of the "messianic-secret" phenomenon becomes visible only when it is reconceptualized as a hermeneutical phenomenon: the obscure but normative text and its clarifying exposition. As such a phenomenon, Wrede recognizes its course from Mark via John to Gnosticism:

> Jesus speaks his lucid and simple parables without having any other intention than what is a matter of course to every speaker. The first Christian who to our knowledge narrates his life already betrays a lack of any understanding for the meaning of this form of discourse. The parables are already mysterious words, for which a key is needed. Yet he and his successors do not yet in the least have in mind to entice from them teachings that were higher than other teachings of Jesus, as the very rarity of interpretations indicates. In John the genuine parables have all but disappeared, and the aspect of a puzzle is in a certain sense attached to Jesus' whole manner of teaching. But finally the whole traditional teaching, as present in the now completed Gospels, is stamped as *parabolē*, unintelligible mystery, in order, with a polite gesture, to push it to one side.[27]

Wrede finds the two levels of teaching to be explicitly cast by Gnosticism in terms of two periods of time, corresponding to Jesus' earthly and exalted modes of being. But, apart from the "gnostic" church father Clement of Alexandria ("To James the Just and Peter and John the Lord transmitted the *gnosis* after the resurrection"[28]), Wrede must move toward the end of the third century to document in Gnosticism "the subsequent history of the concept," in *Pistis Sophia*:[29] Having passed eleven years with the disciples after the resurrection, without revealing the highest truths, Jesus ascends and then returns to them transfigured by light, to say: "Rejoice and be glad from this hour because I have been to the places from whence I came forth. From today onwards now I will speak with you openly (*parrhēsia*) from the beginning of the truth until its completion. And I will speak with you from face to face, without parable (*parabolē*). I will not conceal from you, from this hour onwards, anything of the

---

[27]*Messiasgeheimnis*, pp. 250–251 (ET, pp. 251–252).
[28]*Messiasgeheimnis*, p. 246 (ET, p. 247), citing Eusebius, II, 1.
[29]*Messiasgeheimnis*, pp. 248–249 (ET, 249–250).

things of the height and of the place of truth."[30] Here, to be sure, it was the eleven years between resurrection and ascension in which Jesus, having resumed his earthly life, had failed to communicate the higher revelation, rather than the public ministry, which is fully ignored. But there is a clear chronological cleavage between the two levels of instruction, corresponding to Jesus' two successive modes of being, before and after his ascension. Here one can see how in Gnosticism the shift in modes of his speaking, originally localized at Easter where the shift in modes of being had been placed, could be moved forward in time as the shift in modes of being came to be shifted forward.

Even the vocabulary used in *Pistis Sophia* to describe the two levels is significant: "in parables" (*parabolē*) and "openly" (*parrhēsia*). For this is in substance the vocabulary employed by John, even though he uses instead of *parabolē* the similar term *paroimia*: "I have said this to you in figures (*paroimia*); the hour is coming when I shall no longer speak to you in figures (*paroimia*) but tell you plainly (*parrhēsia*) of the Father. . . . I came from the Father and have come into the world; again, I am leaving the world and going to the Father. His disciples said, Ah, now you are speaking plainly (*parrhēsia*), not in any figure (*paroimia*)!" (John 16:25, 28, 29). Here the two levels of meaning recur, though again not divided precisely by the resurrection, but rather by the point at which the substance of the resurrection had been relocated, in this case back to the parting discourses—a time which for John is in substance one with the exaltation (17:1: "Father, the hour has come . . ."). It is significant that John uses this same term (*paroimia*) to refer to a parable, and in that instance too there is the concept that parabolic language is unintelligible: "This figure (*paroimia*) Jesus used with them, but they did not understand what he was saying to them" (John 10:6)—whereupon follows the interpretation ("I am the door. . . . I am the good shepherd. . . .").

Thus we find in John an association of the chronological distinction between obscure and clear with the concept of parable and its interpreta-

---

[30]*Die griechischen christlichen Schriftsteller der ersten drei Jahrhunderte: Koptisch-gnostische Schriften*, Vol. 1, ed. Carl Schmidt and Walter Till (1959), p. 5,31–38, from ch. 6. Cf. also ch. 88, p. 130,17, ch. 90, p. 132,2–3, ch. 100, p. 159,6: "reveal without parable." The specific references were collected by M. Malinine, H.-C. Peuch, G. Quispel, and W. Till, ed., in *De Resurrectione* (1963), p. 25 to 45,6–8. For the Coptic text and English translation see Carl Schmidt and Violet MacDermot, *Pistis Sophia*, The Coptic Gnostic Library, Nag Hammadi Studies 9 (1978), pp. 8, 21–9, 4 from ch. 6; cf. also ch. 88, p. 202, 5, ch. 90, p. 204, 19–20, ch. 100, p. 248, 3.

tion, as well as a substantive shift in the point of time from Easter back into Jesus' life. Now this same cluster of interrelated ingredients recurs in Mark. Its roots go back to the pre-Marcan collection imbedded in Mark 4:1–34. This pre-Marcan collection had the concept of parables as riddles, intended for outsiders, and then "privately resolved for his own disciples" (4:34).[31] This original hermeneutical function of the parable's interpretation is however obscured by Mark himself, in that the disciples, in spite of the interpretation, remain as much in the dark as do the outsiders (Mark 4:13; 8:17–21). Mark himself takes over the hermeneutical concept of hidden and open levels of meaning current in the parable tradition (and in *The Gospel of Thomas,* Saying 1), and locates his own shift from one level to the other at the first prediction of the passion and resurrection, to which the comment is appended (Mark 8:32): "And he spoke the word plainly *(parrhēsia).*" Here we have, from Mark's point of view, the turning point substantively equivalent to the resurrection (much as for John the parting discourses were the coming of the hour equivalent to the exaltation, and as for *Pistis Sophia, mutatis mutandis,* the ascension, after eleven years of postresurrection earthly togetherness, marks via luminous transfiguration the moment when the higher truth of the exalted one is communicated). That is to say that the basic chronological divide can be shifted forward or backward from the third day, if theological considerations tend to move forward or backward the revelatory event which brings the higher interpretation.

If for *Pistis Sophia* (like Luke-Acts) the resurrection is a resumption of earthly life and first the ascension produces the basic change (cf. the gift of the Spirit first at the ascension on Pentecost), then the two levels of meaning can be distributed in such a way that the whole earthly period, including resurrection appearances of an earthly kind such as one has at the end of the Gospels, can be equated with the unintelligible or literal text, and hence the period of higher revelation takes place only with the

---

[31]The hermeneutical technical term of "resolving" or supplying a "resolution" of parables as riddles recurs in the *Similitudes of Hermas* and *Pistis Sophia.* This is a small indication of the continuity of tradition along the trajectory here being traced. Similar hermeneutical terms for connecting text and interpretation are "teaching" (Did. 3,1) and "pesher" (Qumran); cf. my essay "LOGOI SOPHŌN: Zur Gattung der Spruchquelle Q," *Zeit und Geschichte,* Bultmann *Festschrift* (1964), p. 85, republished in enlarged English version as "LOGOI SOPHŌN: On the *Gattung* of Q," in *The Future of Our Religious Past: Essays in Honour of Rudolf Bultmann,* ed. James M. Robinson (1971), p. 100, and in *Trajectories through Early Christianity,* p. 86.

ascension, where the transfiguration into luminous existence first takes place. In the case of Mark and John, where the basic turning point is from an aretalogical public ministry to a kerygmatic crucifixion, the beginning of the period of higher revelation can be transplanted back from the resurrection appearances to the point at which the passion narrative is thematically initiated: Mark 8 and John 16. Here one can sense a turning away from a potentially gnostic theology of resurrection toward something more like a *theologia crucis*, as Jesus' open "word" (Mark) or "glorification" (John). If gnostics can deny the higher more normative authority even to resurrection appearances in which Jesus resumes earthly life, so as to deny ultimacy to such earthly life, John and Mark point in the opposite direction toward emergent orthodoxy in placing that ultimacy back into the life of Jesus and thereby providing a theological rationale for transmitting the traditions of his earthly life, so as in effect to engender the *Gattung* Gospel.

The orthodox church, in spite of its appropriation of the canonical Gospel *Gattung*, and thus the obscuring of the original chronological separation of the two levels of understanding at Easter, did preserve vestiges of that earlier view, in the orthodox form of its orientation to the kerygma of cross and resurrection. Luke, in spite of the fading of the messianic secret and of the *theologia crucis* from his theology, attests the tradition in question quite clearly.[32] The view, shared by the disciples, that Jesus was a miracle-working prophet (Luke 7:16; 24:19), whose career would culminate in a national deliverance (Luke 19:11; 24:21; Acts 1:6), is lifted to a higher plane after the resurrection (even though the resurrected Jesus is portrayed in very earthly terms). This takes the form of opening their eyes to the kerygmatic meaning of the Old Testament (Luke 24:25–27, 32, 44–47), which is the hermeneutical equivalent to the gift of the Spirit. Furthermore, this Easter shift is insured against the possibility—exploited by Gnosticism—of relegating to insignificance the early earthly life of Jesus, as just a lower and hence irrelevant prelude. For Luke 24:44 adds: "These are my words which I spoke to you, while I was still with you . . ."

This is precisely the orthodox combination attested also by Justin.[33] After the disciples saw the resurrected one, were initiated by him into kerygmatic exegesis of the Old Testament, and had witnessed the ascension

---

[32]Cf. *Messiasgeheimnis*, pp. 240–242 (ET, pp. 241–243).
[33]*Messiasgeheimnis*, pp. 243–245 (ET, pp. 245–247).

and received power from on high, from *then* on they taught the Christian message and were called apostles (Apol. I,50). The *Dialogue with Trypho*, 106, like Luke, adds to these minimum requirements for the Easter reversal the stipulation that the disciples acknowledge that even before his suffering Jesus had predicted the kerygma. Thus, the chronological divide at Easter, potentially a threat to the revelatory nature of all that went before, is domesticated in such a way as to preserve both the Old Testament and the earthly ministry of Jesus, that is, the orthodox gospel *Gattung* within a nascent Christian canon.

Gnosticism, in turn, preferred the exalted Christ, no doubt because he has seen the heavens and is freed from a body, and hence is more qualified to give gnostic revelations than was the earthly Jesus. But even though Gnosticism's Gospel *Gattung* begins just as regularly after the resurrection as the orthodox *Gattung* ends there, the gnostic still wanted to claim for gnostic teaching the earthly Jesus as well[34]—somewhat as, conversely, the orthodox church claimed the teaching of the resurrected for orthodoxy. In *The Letter of Peter to Philip* (NH VIII,2), when the disciples pose to the resurrected their gnostic questions on "'the (Mount) of Olives,' the place where they used to gather with the blessed Christ when he was in the body" (133:15–17), Jesus begins his answer by observing (135:5–8): "It is you yourselves who are witnesses that I spoke all these things to you. But because of your unbelief I shall speak again."[35] Here we have in effect the two levels of interpretation, the unbelieved text of the earthly Jesus and the believed repetition, that is, the intelligible gnostic interpretation by the resurrected. Gnostics, like the orthodox, validated their post-Easter doctrines by attributing them to the (uncomprehended) teachings of the earthly Jesus, to whom a potentially revelatory role could thus be conceded.

*The Apocryphon of James* from the Jung Codex (NH I,2) is considerably earlier (second century) and less gnostic than *Pistis Sophia*. It holds a mediating position between the bifurcating orthodox and gnostic positions, and supplements from a somewhat gnostic side what has been seen in Luke and Justin from the orthodox side. Indeed the opening framework

---

[34]Cf. *Excerpta ex Theodoto*, 66: "The savior taught the apostles, the first things typically and mystically, the later things parabolically and enigmatically, the third things clearly and patiently in private." These periods may correspond respectively to the Old Testament, the public ministry, and the resurrection.

[35]135:5–8. Cf. also 137:28; 138:3; 138:22–27; 139:11–12.

may refer equally well to both kinds of Gospel, in describing (2:10–15) the disciples after the resurrection as "recalling what the Savior had said to each one of them, whether in secret or openly, and [setting it in order] in books." In any case, there is a depreciation of those who were with the earthly Jesus, in view of their being still "drunk": "Remember that you have seen the Son of Man, and spoken with him in person and listened to him in person. Woe to those who have (only) seen the son of man. Blessed will they be who have not seen the man, and they who have not consorted with him and have not spoken with him and have not heard anything from him . . .; yours is life!" (3:12–25). "Blessed will they be who have known me; woe to those who have heard and have not believed" (12:38–40). This is strikingly similar to the Johannine blessing, not on Thomas, but on those who do not see and yet believe (20:29).

The contrast between two levels of understanding also occurs in formulations analogous to Mark. When Jesus says (5:33–35), "Remember my cross and my death, and you will live," James replies (5:36—6:1), "Lord, do not mention to us the cross and death, for they are far from you," to which Jesus retorts (6:2–4), "Verily I say unto you, none will be saved unless they believe in my cross." This is strikingly similar to the confrontation at Caesarea Philippi (Mark 8:31–33), where it is pointedly said Jesus spoke openly *(parrhēsia)*, even though the disciples in fact continue to misunderstand. Similarly *The Apocryphon of James* (7:1–6): "At first I spoke with you in parables *(parabolē)* and you did not understand; now I speak to you openly, and you (still) do not perceive." Eager to ascend, the resurrected complains (8:1–4): "For after the [end] you have compelled me to stay with you another eighteen days[36] for the sake of the parables." Parables are actually listed. But it is not clear whether the delay is so that the parables may be interpreted during the eighteen days or months, or whether, as in *Pistis Sophia,* the resumption of earthly life between resurrection and ascension is still on the level of obscurity (9:32–33: "Can you still bear to sleep?"). In any case the climax of the narration is the spiritual ascent of James and Peter following the ascending savior, which first seems to achieve the actual revelation (15:38; 16:4, 25).

---

[36]Since 18 days seems an arbitrary figure, whereas the 550 days of 2:19 corresponds approximately to the 18 months of sojourn after the resurrection attested elsewhere, one may conjecture that the interchangeability of calculation by day and by month led to the error of 18 days rather than 18 months or 550 days.

## On the Gattung of Mark (and John)

### B. The Turning Point of the Gattung Gospel

The move on Mark's part to transfer the "Easter" shift to 8:32 is less drastic, more comparable to John's placing it at 16:25, 29, when one recognizes that Mark's reference to Jesus now teaching openly is not only a commentary upon the first prediction of the passion (8:31), itself a passion narrative in miniature, but is followed by the transfiguration (9:2–8). For this has often[37] been conjectured to have been originally a resurrection appearance, as 9:9 seems vaguely to sense: "As they were coming down the mountain, he charged them to tell no one what they had seen, until the son of man should have risen from the dead." This assessment of the transfiguration story as originally a resurrection appearance is of course contested. Certainly the transfiguration is not comparable to the resurrection appearances with which the canonical Gospels conclude, in which Jesus is not transformed away from normal human appearance, but, quite the contrary, is recognizable by his wounds (John 20:20, 25, 27), or is mistakable for another human, such as a gardener (John 20:15) or traveller (Luke 24:16, 18), or fisherman (John 21:4).

Yet in gnostic Gospels, cast normally in the framework of resurrection appearances,[38] a luminous apparition comparable to the transfiguration is the rule. In *Pistis Sophia* 2–3, a great luminous power[39] descends upon Jesus after 11 years, darkening the disciples' eyes, who saw only the light; the light then takes Jesus up to heaven, and he returns, luminous, for the revelation. In *The Letter of Peter to Philip* (NH VIII, 2), the resurrected appeared as "a great light" (134:10), from which the voice of the resurrected speaks. In *The Apocryphon of James* (NH I,2), when at the end of the 550 days Jesus is to ascend, he calls upon James and Peter (14:25–26, 35–36) to "pay heed to the glory that awaits me . . . from now I shall strip myself in order that I may clothe myself"—an obvious reference to seeing him in glory, as light. *The Apocryphon of John*, known from P. Berol. 8502 prior to the discovery of three additional copies at Nag Hammadi (NH II, *1;* III, *I;* IV, *I*), depicts a bright light appearing from heaven (NH II, *1*:1:33), and Jesus then seen within it (NH II, *1*:2:1–2:7). Also

---

[37]Cf. C. E. Carlston, "Transfiguration and Resurrection," *JBL* 80 (1961): 233–240; Ernst Käsemann, *RGG,* 3rd ed., 6 (1962), 1835.

[38]Cf. Hennecke's *New Testament Apocrypha,* ed. Wilhelm Schneemelcher, ET by R. McL. Wilson, (1963), pp. 82, 188–230, 246.

[39]Cf. the cloud that takes him away in Acts 1:9; in Epistula Apostolorum, 51 (62) (*New Testament Apocrypha,* I, p. 227) it is a "bright cloud" that takes him away.

the *Sophia of Jesus Christ* was known from P. Berol. 8502, and has been supplemented by an additional copy from Nag Hammadi (NH III,4). Here too the resurrected appears "like a great angel of light" (NH III,4:91:13), the significance of which is also made explicit (NH III,4:93:8–12): "I am here. For I am he who knows it (the Light), so that I might speak to you concerning the precise nature of the truth." In *Thomas the Contender* (NH II,7) this purpose is even more explicit. Thomas says to the resurrected (139:20), "You, our light, enlighten, Lord!" To this Jesus replies (139:21), "It is in light that light exists." Thomas then calls for further explication (139:22–24): "Lord, why does this visible light that shines on behalf of men rise and set?" The reply is given (141:25–30): "O blessed Thomas, of course this visible light shone on your behalf—not in order that you remain here but rather that you come forth—and whenever all the elect abandon bestiality, then this light will withdraw up to its essence."

It is the rule that these gnostic appearances of the resurrected in light take place on a mountain (PS 2; P. Berol. 2: 20:1; P. Berol. 3: 77:16; NH V,2: 30:19; NH VIII,2: 133:14).[40] At the time 2 Peter was composed, its reference in 1:16–18 to the apostles being "eye-witnesses of his majesty," "when he received honor and glory from God" "on the holy mountain," would most naturally have been taken as a reference to a resurrection appearance. For not only was being a witness to the resurrection the basic qualification for apostleship, and the traditional dating for Jesus receiving honor and glory the resurrection (cf. Matt. 28:18–20); the luminous glory coming on the resurrected Jesus on the mountain was so common, if not within the orthodox circles of 2 Peter, then in those of such off-beat Christian movements as he was combatting, that the appeal to the resurrected to accredit 2 Peter would be unmistakable. Yet the reference is equally applicable to the transfiguration.

Perhaps we here strike upon an early Christian tradition not exclusively gnostic, but suppressed in orthodox Christianity, and surviving in the New Testament canon only indirectly, at mislocated positions, having

---

[40]The Coptic fragments of an apocryphal Gospel in the Strasbourg library seem to be a further instance, though the fragmentary nature of the remains makes any final judgment impossible. One fragment, apparently the conclusion, refers to Jesus "revealing my whole glory;" and contains a phrase after a lacuna about being on a "mountain." *New Testament Apocrypha*, I, pp. 227–230.

yielded the official position at the end of the Gospels to the nonluminous human appearances. Paul's conversion is an encounter with a blinding light, which according to Luke's chronology falls outside the period of resurrection appearances. Perhaps even earlier the appearance to Peter, because of its luminosity, ceded its position within the accepted period of resurrection appearances, and, rather than being simply lost, found a new location as the transfiguration story, which is clearly the same scene as that to which 2 Peter 1:16–18 refers. Surely gnostics could, for example, in their depreciation of bodily existence, interpret such a primitive Christian visualization of resurrection[41] in their own gnostic categories, which, however, were presumably not those of the earlier instances. The fact that Gnosticism is not the only context in which they could occur is attested in Rev. 1:12ff., where Christ appears with his face "like the sun shining in full strength" (1:16).

Thus the turning point in Mark's Gospel, no longer explainable in terms of a turning point in the life of the historical Jesus and thereby redefined as a problem of Marcan composition, may find its explanation in his intent, part and parcel with his intent in writing the Gospel, to transfer the authority previously reserved for the resurrected back into the life of the earthly Jesus, elevating it to the authoritative position that justifies the Marcan *Gattung* Gospel.

## C. *The Beginning Point of the* Gattung *Gospel*

In view of the fact that Mark has perhaps been related to apocalypticism[42] more often than to Gnosticism, it may be relevant in conclusion to draw attention to a further instance where the Nag Hammadi materials and apocalypticism join in clarifying the structure of Mark, in this instance its beginning. It is not in itself surprising to begin a Gospel with John the Baptist, for, *pace* Matthew and Luke, it was the dominant concept in the first phase of Gospel-writing: Q, the Miracles Source used by John, Mark, John; even Luke succeeds in paying lip service to that tradition by beginning his infancy narrative with John. Such a widespread consensus as to where a Gospel should begin can be explained most simply by

---

[41]Cf., for example, 1 Cor. 15:40–43; 2 Cor. 3:18; Phil. 3:21.

[42]Cf. Willi Marxsen, *Der Evangelist Markus* (1956), and my book of the same year, *The Problem of History in Mark* (Studies in Biblical Theology 21), where I already refer (p. 28) to Rev. 12 in relation to the opening of Mark.

reference to Jesus' own pointing to John as the turning-point (Q: Matt. 11:12–13 par.) The Lucan definition of an apostle as having begun from the baptism of John (*sic* Acts 1:22), and his definition of the public ministry as beginning from Galilee after the baptism which John preached (Acts 10:37), reflect such a tradition.[43] Thus it is in itself not surprising that Mark should begin here. Yet the varying ways in which beginning from John is implemented in the Gospels indicate that the actual details of the Marcan beginning are not to be derived from that tradition alone.[44] *The Apocalypse of Adam* from Nag Hammadi (NH V,5) seems to provide the nearest parallels, to be a missing link to other parallels, and to put in profile some of the otherwise obscure details.

The last part of *The Apocalypse of Adam* consists of thirteen brief stories of the coming of the Illuminator, all of which follow the same outline. By placing these stories side by side one can see clearly the outline, in spite of various exceptions, and identify the cluster of relatively interchangeable alternatives available at each stage of the story. The quotation of two typical instances (78:6–17, 18–26), and then the listing of the items in the outline, will make the structure clear.

(1) And the second kingdom says about him (2) that he came from a great prophet. (6) And a bird came, took the child who was born and brought him onto a high mountain. (7) And he was nourished by the bird of heaven. An angel came forth there. He said to him: "Arise! God has given glory to you." (8) He received glory and strength. (9) And thus he came to the water.

(1) The third kingdom says of him (2) that he came from a virgin womb. (6) He was cast out of his city, he and his mother; he was brought to a desert place. (7) He was nourished there. (8) He came and received glory and power. (9) And thus he came to the water.

(1) The stereotyped quotation formula: "The 'n'th kingdom says of him."

(2) The coming of the illuminator: He came from a great prophet (the second kingdom); or from a virgin womb (the third kingdom; cf. also the fourth kingdom); or from a drop from heaven (the fifth kingdom; cf. also the seventh kingdom: he is a drop which came from heaven to earth); or from a cloud enveloping a rock (the eighth kingdom); from one of the nine Muses (the ninth kingdom); or from two illuminators (the twelfth kingdom); or

---

[43]Cf. William C. Robinson, Jr., *Der Weg des Herrn: Studien zur Geschichte und Eschatologie im Lukas-Evangelium*, Theologische Forschung 36 (1964): p. 33.

[44]Cf. my concession, *The Problem of History in Mark*, below, p. 75, of an inability to find a specific history-of-religions context for this narrative.

from a foreign air, from a great aeon (the generation without a king, that is, the true view).

(3) Lust involved in the illuminator's conception (since not all the stories are *birth* stories—in some the illuminator simply comes—, obviously items 3–5, lust, pregnancy, and birth are not always present): There is the desire of the flowers (the sixth kingdom); or a Muse desired herself (the ninth kingdom); or the illuminator's god loved a cloud of desire (the tenth kingdom); or the father desired his own daughter (the eleventh kingdom); or there was a desire of the "powers" (the thirteenth kingdom). In one instance (the fourth kingdom) a lustful campaign is narrated (78:30—79:10): "Solomon sought her, he and Phersalo and Sauel and his armies which had been sent out. Solomon himself sent his army of demons to seek out the virgin. And they did not find the one whom they sought, but the virgin who was given to them. It was she whom they fetched. Solomon took her."

(4) The pregnancy of the woman: Of course, the Solomon story (the fourth kingdom) continues (79:10–11): "The virgin became pregnant." This motif recurs in most of the stories where the lust motif is present (the sixth, ninth, and eleventh kingdoms).

(5) The child was born (the ninth and tenth kingdoms); or the mother gave birth to him (the fourth and sixth kingdoms).

(6) Some kind of removal of the illuminator: once along with his mother (the third kingdom), to a desert place (the third, fourth, and eleventh kingdoms); or "a bird came, took the child who was born and brought him onto a high mountain" (the second kingdom); or "a spirit came upon him and brought him on high to the place where the drop had come forth" (the seventh kingdom; cf. also the first kingdom). Sometimes the removal to the place of refuge is not stated, but a vestigial remnant of such a motif is present, in saying the mother gave birth to him "in that place;" or some such vestigial trait is attached to one of the next items.

(7) The child is nourished: The mother nourished him in heaven (the first kingdom) or on a border of the desert (the fourth kingdom); he was nourished by a bird of heaven (the second kingdom) or by the angels (the sixth, eighth, and eleventh kingdoms).

(8) The refrain: "He received glory and power." Once (the second kingdom) the ceremony of receiving glory and strength is also spelled out: "An angel came forth there. He said to him: 'Arise! God has given glory to you.'"

(9) The summary of the narrative with the phrase: "And thus he came to the water."

Items (1), (2), (8), and (9), that is, the formal framework, are present almost without exception; other items, where the materials of each individual story play some role, involve omissions, expansions, fusions, and other irregularities, and yet there is a remarkable degree of regularity.

In studying this outline of the Jewish-gnostic *Apocalypse of Adam,* one immediately thinks of the mythological birth narrative in the Christian-apocalyptic Apocalypse of John (Revelation 12). Here the mother is "a woman clothed with the sun, with the moon under her feet" (12:1). This may be equivalent to the view of the twelfth kingdom, that the redeemer "came from two illuminators." These may be the two illuminators of Genesis 1, the sun and the moon, for the same term (Phostēr) is used in the LXX, *The Apocalypse of Adam,* and Revelation 12. Most of the nine items in the outline do occur in Revelation 12:

(4) This mythological woman is pregnant (Rev. 12:2): "She was with child and she cried out in her pangs of birth, in anguish for delivery."

(5) Then (12:5a) she gave birth to a boy.

(6) Next (12:5b–6) occurs the removal to a high or desert place, although now the options are divided between the child and his mother: "Her child was caught up to God and to his throne, and the woman fled into the wilderness, where she has a place prepared by God."

(7) Next comes the nourishing—not of the child, but rather of the mother: She is "nourished for 1260 days" (12:6).

(8) Although there is no statement that the infant received glory and power, one may recall that in one instance (the second kingdom) in *The Apocalypse of Adam* this item is in narrative form: "Arise! God has given glory to you." There is a somewhat similar narration in Rev. 12:10: "A loud voice in heaven" is heard saying in hymnic style: "Now the salvation and the power and the kingdom of our God and the authority of his Christ have come . . ."

(3) To be sure there is no mention of lust, but this is often the case in *The Apocalypse of Adam* as well. Since it is usually present in birth narratives there, one may attribute its absence here to the apocalypticist's prudity. Once (the fourth kingdom) in *The Apocalypse of Adam* this motif became a lustful campaign between two armies. In Rev. 12 there is also a battle, though not related to lust for the virgin. A "great, red dragon" is ready to "devour her child when she brought it forth" (12:3–4). Then (12:7–9) "war arose in heaven, Michael and his angels fighting against the dragon; and the dragon and his angels fought" and lost, and the dragon was thrown down to the earth with his army of angels.

There is a flashback to the birth of the child (Rev. 12:13), which leads to a repetition also of the removal, though of the mother only (Rev. 12:14): "But the woman was given the two wings of the great eagle that she might fly from the serpent into the wilderness, to the place. . . ." Thus the mother in effect becomes a bird, just as once (the second kingdom) in *The Apocalypse of Adam* "a bird came, took the child who was born and brought him onto a high mountain." Item 8 in the outline, "thus he came to the water," is not present in Revelation 12, although the story ends (12:15) with the serpent pouring water like a river out of his mouth to sweep the woman away with the flood; she is saved (12:16) by the earth swallowing the river.

In view of the striking parallels between Revelation 12 and the thirteen stories of the coming of the illuminator in *The Apocalypse of Adam* (especially the core of the birth stories, namely the sequence of pregnancy, birth, removal, and nourishing), there must be some relation between the two documents. Although Revelation 12 is a mythological presentation of the birth of the Christian redeemer, the difficulties that the history of exegesis has had in correlating the specifics of the story with the infancy narratives (for example, the identification of the mother with Mary), indicate that Revelation 12 cannot be explained as derived from the facts of Jesus' birth or even from the traditions about his birth in or behind Matthew and Luke. Rather, Revelation 12 seems to be using mythological traditions that have only in part been Christianized, and which hence only haltingly lend themselves to the exegete's *interpretatio christiana*. Hence it is improbable that the tradition developed in the following sequence: Jesus' historical birth; legends about it such as we have in Matthew and Luke; the mythologizing of it as in Revelation 12; then borrowing by *The Apocalypse of Adam*. Nor is Revelation 12 clearly dependent on *The Apocalypse of Adam*. Hence it is probably correct to assume they shared traditions which *The Apocalypse of Adam* rigidified into a rather pat outline and *The Apocalypse of John* Christianized to a certain extent.

One can to some degree infer what the basic ingredients in the traditions were, and on this basis identify secondary traits. Since the story has to do with the birth or coming of a redeemer, interest focuses on him, and the mother is incidental—indeed is usually absent, when it is not a matter of a *birth* story, but only of the illuminator's *coming*. Hence it is the illuminator that is removed and nourished. Thus the version in Revelation 12 that the infant is taken to heaven and God's throne, while the woman is taken to the wilderness, seems to be a secondary splitting up of the action. This is probably due to Christian influence, namely the idea of Christ's ascension, and the association of the woman (at least at this point in the story) with the church militant: the dragon makes war on "the rest of her offspring" (12:17). A further variation between the two documents is that in Revelation 12 it is the woman who is nourished, whereas in *The Apocalypse of Adam* it is always the child. Indeed, in a birth narrative interest would normally center on the birth, protection, and nourishment of the child, rather than on the mother. But the ascended Christ hardly needs feeding. Thus slight variations in Revelation 12 from the basically non-Christian apocalyptic story betray the Christianizing process beginning to operate.

Whereas Revelation 12 preserves the myth largely in its non-Christian form, with only peripheral Christianizing ingredients (cf. also 12:10,17), the same myth recurs in *The Gospel of the Hebrews*,[45] in this instance with a stronger ingredient of Christian traditions. One fragment reads: "When Christ wished to come upon the earth to men, the good Father summoned a mighty power in heaven, which was called Michael, and entrusted Christ to the care thereof."[46] Here the coming is accompanied by the same Michael who fights for mother and child in Revelation 12. In *The Gospel of the Hebrews* Michael is incarnated as Mary, in whose womb Christ stayed for seven months.

Another fragment of *The Gospel of the Hebrews* reports the savior saying: "Even so did my mother, the Holy Spirit, take me by one of my hairs and carry me away on to the great mountain Tabor." In *The Apocalypse of Adam* the first kingdom narrates similarly that a spirit took the illuminator to heaven to be nourished on "the bosom of his mother" (78:4), who in the parallel is identified with the Spirit. Similar, though less close parallels occur in other instances of the story: According to the seventh kingdom it is also a spirit that takes him on high; according to the ninth kingdom one of the nine Muses takes him to a high mountain; according to the second kingdom it is a bird which takes him to the high mountain. The flight of a bird is suggested in *The Gospel of the Hebrews* by the image of the mother taking the infant to the mountain by one of his hairs. In Rev. 12:14 the woman is given wings to fly like a bird to refuge. Thus, although any identification of the woman of Revelation 12 with the Holy Spirit is no more than one interpretation (Pétrement) among others, and hence the

---

[45]Cf. P. Vielhauer in Schneemelcher, ed., *New Testament Apocrypha*, I, pp. 158–65.

[46]On the question of whether this fragment actually derives from the Gospel of the Hebrews, cf. Vielhauer, *New Testament Apocrypha*, I, pp. 137, 160.

parallel is not complete, there are several interlocking ingredients that suggest shared traditions.

A still further fragment of *The Gospel of the Hebrews* reads: "And it came to pass when the Lord was come up out of the water, the whole fount of the Holy Spirit descended upon him and rested on him and said to him: My Son, in all the prophets was I waiting for thee that thou shouldest come and I might rest in thee. For thou art my rest; thou art my first-begotten Son that reignest for ever." Here one has, in terms of the coming of the Spirit, the gnostic redeemer myth in the form Rudolf Bultmann first identified it, namely as the Sophia myth of Jewish literature. In Enoch 42:1–2 Sophia sought a resting place on earth, but found it in Judaism and the Torah; in *The Gospel of the Hebrews* this resting place is Christ. Furthermore, in *The Gospel of the Hebrews,* as in *The Apocalypse of Adam,* there is a coming on the water. But it is not Jesus who comes on the water; rather it is the Spirit who comes on him, as he is coming up out of the water at his baptism.

In these varying ways *The Gospel of the Hebrews* has taken the materials of the traditional myth as we find it in *The Apocalypse of Adam* and Revelation 12 and fitted elements of it into Christian traditions of Jesus' birth and baptism, a merger in which the mythological ingredient still asserts itself strongly.

It is somewhat surprising, in view of the birth narratives that occur in a number of instances in *The Apocalypse of Adam* and Revelation 12, and in view of the allusion to the mother in one of the fragments of *The Gospel of the Hebrews,* that in *The Gospel of the Hebrews* the myth is merged with the Christian baptism story rather than with an infancy narrative. Perhaps there was also some baptism association of the myth implicit in *The Apocalypse of Adam* itself, such as might be suggested by the designation of the elect seed as "those who will receive his name on the water" (83:5–6). Since the stories in *The Apocalypse of Adam* are basically of the *coming* of the redeemer, and not necessarily by means of *birth,* the myth could have attached itself to the Christian tradition at the point where the Christian story originally opened, that is, at the baptism, especially when there was no infancy narrative in a given tradition to provide another alternative.

This immediately draws attention to the Marcan narrative itself. Perhaps this context can shed some light on how the baptism and temptation material was brought together to provide the first story about the coming of Jesus as Son of God. Mark 1:9–13 does present some possible points of contact, which when taken together strengthen the likelihood that the Christian tradition and the non-Christian myth meet here, though with the Christian tradition predominating considerably more than was the case in Revelation 12 and *The Gospel of the Hebrews*. Such a comparison makes more intelligible and meaningful the Marcan presentation itself, and on that ground also commends itself.

Mark 1:9: "In those days Jesus came from Nazareth of Galilee and was baptized by John in the Jordan." Here the first motif of the stories of *The Apocalypse of Adam*, the fact of the coming of the illuminator, and the last motif, the retrospective allusion to him coming on the water, have either been replaced or historicized by the tradition that Jesus came to be baptized by John in the Jordan. But there is also a coming from heaven:

Mark 1:10 "And when he came up out of the water, immediately he saw the heavens opened and the Spirit descending upon him like a dove." Hence, as in *The Gospel of the Hebrews*, the coming from heaven is the descent of the Spirit on Jesus at the Jordan waters, rather than a descent of Jesus. Perhaps this double coming in Mark, the "historical" coming of Jesus from Galilee to the Jordan, and the "mythological" coming of the Spirit from heaven on Jesus in the water, is an adjustment of Christian tradition with the non-Christian story, comparable to the double removal in Revelation 12 of the child to heaven and the mother to the desert. The description of the Spirit as a dove may reflect the birdlike associations of the mother or Spirit in the texts analyzed thus far.

Mark 1:11 "And a voice came from heaven, Thou art my beloved son; with thee I am well pleased." One recalls the motif in *The Apocalypse of Adam* of the redeemer receiving glory and power, which once was expanded with the angel's voice addressing him: "Arise! God has given glory to you." We have already compared this with the absence in Revelation 12 of a statement that he received glory and power, but the presence (12:10–12) of the narration that a loud voice in heaven said: "Now the salvation and the power and the kingdom of our God and the authority of his Christ have come . . ."

Mark 1:12 "And the Spirit immediately drove him out into the wilderness." Twice in *The Apocalypse of Adam* (the first and seventh kingdoms) it is a spirit that removed the redeemer—to heaven in these instances, although the predominant place to which he is removed in *The Apocalypse of Adam* is the desert. In *The Gospel of the Hebrews*, the Spirit removed him to a great mountain (Tabor), reminiscent of the Q temptation narrative partly located on a very high mountain (Matt. 4:8 par.).

Mark 1:13: "And he was with the wild beasts; and the angels ministered to him." In *The Apocalypse of Adam* it is usually angels who nourish the illuminator (according to the sixth, eighth, and eleventh kingdoms). It has been conjectured that the "wild beasts" of Mark 1:13 are intended as hostile. *The Apocalypse of Adam* does not emphasize a specific danger from which one is removed to be nourished. But Revelation 12:3,7,9 does introduce at this point the dragon or serpent; its identification with the devil and Satan (12:9,12) may be a link between the baptism and temptation in Q, where the devil and Satan replace, so to speak, the wild beasts (Matt. 4:1,5,10,11 par.). Q also presents Jesus fasting, becoming hungry, and then being tempted to change stones into bread (Matt. 4:2–4 par.). The issue in Q then becomes who will nourish or minister (food) to Jesus, the devil or the angels (Matt. 4:11 par.). Thus we see at the opening of Mark (and Q) a series of traits similar to those in the stories of the coming of the redeemer. This does not mean the stories of Jesus' baptism and temptation originated from the mythological story we have traced; rather the parallels would help to explain how and why Mark brought together certain incidents from the Christian tradition to fill out his composition, as well as perhaps explaining the origin of certain peculiarities in the way the Marcan story is told.

## II

# GNOSTICISM AND THE
# NEW TESTAMENT

We wish to turn in our survey of the potential impact of the Nag Hammadi codices on New Testament studies to that less obvious pendant to John, namely the Gospel of Mark, as New Testament scholarship has been taught to understand it by the remarkably insightful work with which the study of the Gospels in our century began, William Wrede's *Das Messiasgeheimnis in den Evangelien.* "If one looks at Mark with a powerful magnifying glass, one has something like the kind of literary activity that John exemplifies."[1] Whereas at that time the Synoptic Gospels stood over against the Gospel of John, in that the former were source material for the quest of the historical Jesus in a way the latter was not, Wrede demonstrated the shocking extent to which Mark and John are nearer theologically to each other than is either to Matthew and Luke, and precisely because of a trajectory they share with Gnosticism.[2]

Wrede was able to mock up the Gnostic outcome of this trajectory by reference only to Clement of Alexandria, Pistis Sophia (which he knew only through Harnack's report) and the Codex Brucianus (which Carl Schmidt had translated in 1892; his translation of Pistis Sophia would appear only in 1925). Clearly Wrede lacked such breadth of source material as the Nag Hammadi codices provide.

In fact a substantive weakness in Wrede's presentation is that he is not really able to flesh out a context for the trajectory he intuits. He recognizes that the "secret" is not original with Mark, but hardly can say more:

> Historically the concept is not yet at all intelligible directly from Mark. It is full-grown there. Mark stands under its compulsion, so that one may not even speak [merely] of a "tendency." But where does it come from?—So

[1]W. Wrede, *Das Messiasgeheimnis in den Evangelien,* Göttingen, 1901,²1913,³1963. Eng. tr. by J. C. G. Greig, *The Messianic Secret* (Cambridge and London, 1971). All quotations are my own translation, here from p. 145 (ET, p. 145).
[2]Wrede, *Messiasgeheimnis,* pp. 250–251 (ET, pp. 251–252).

one has to do with a view that must have dominated rather large, though not necessarily quite large circles.[3]

Yet Wrede is not able to clarify the nature of such circles, any more than he was able to fill in the development after Mark. The lack of a discernible context is perhaps related to Wrede's assumption that the "mystery of the person of Jesus" was the *"prius"* among the ingredients in the Marcan theory, which in Wrede's view meant that "for [Mark] the silencings [rather than the theory of parables or the disciples' lack of understanding] must count as the main point."[4] Perhaps the decisive reason for giving priority to the silencings is that Wrede thought that only in this way could he argue that the temporal dimension of resolution at Easter was integral to the whole Messianic secret.

> In the silencings, if we have seen correctly, the thought about the point in time of the resurrection is fundamental. The significance of this point in time cannot be grasped in terms of the view of parables.
>
> Accordingly I consider as the real object of investigation the Messianic self-concealment of Jesus in the nearest and narrowest sense of the word.[5]

Thus it is the role of Easter as a turning point that Wrede perhaps uncritically ascribed to Mark which in turn led him to give priority to one of the three ingredients in the Marcan scheme that then led him to designate the whole phenomenon the Messianic secret.

It is precisely this priority structure that makes the Marcan Messianic secret seem so isolated. Not only does the whole Messianic secret fade in Matthew and Luke, but even John, where close affinity to Mark regarding the Messianic secret in the broader sense is demonstrated, lacks this basic ingredient from which the whole phenomenon receives its name. But in the analysis of John priority is given to the parable theory, whereupon the context for the whole phenomenon and its trajectory begin to emerge:

> The concept of talking in parables has itself experienced an inner transformation . . . The subject of which the Synoptics speak—the real talking in parables itself—has become in John so-to-speak as predicate, a trait of his earthly way of speaking in general . . . I believe rather that it is the *prius* [!]. The original idea was: Jesus spoke on earth in puzzles . . . It receives its sharp formulation in the presentation of teaching the disciples. This is because

---

[3]Wrede, *Messiasgeheimnis*, p. 145 (ET, p. 145).
[4]Wrede, *Messiasgeheimnis*, p. 211 (ET, p. 212).
[5]Wrede, *Messiasgeheimnis*, p. 211 (ET, p. 212).

here it strikes upon the other view from the tradition, namely that the disciples were not able to understand Jesus before his death. This view attracted [that idea of speaking in puzzles] to itself, merged with it and thus first gave it a secure hold . . . The Johannine view could then also stand directly in continuity with a form of the idea that lay behind the Synoptic concept . . . This convergence [of Mark and John] is precisely important since Mark and John are two witnesses that lie rather far apart from each other . . . It proves that we have to do here with ideas that were alive in wider circles of the church.[6]

If thus the Johannine focus is different from what Wrede took to be the center of the Marcan view, but may have pre-Marcan roots and point to a broader context, a somewhat similar trend may be noted when Wrede seeks to trace the subsequent history of the concept. Here too he is compelled to abandon what he had considered the center of the Marcan theory:

> The real idea of the Messianic secret seems to have had only a brief history, just as its area apparently was always limited. Already in the Synoptic successors of Mark it loses its original significance, and in John we no longer encountered it. Elsewhere I cannot turn it up . . . The fact can hardly surprise. It corresponds at least rather well [!] to our interpretation. We have to do not with an idea that would have had a dogmatic or apologetic value in its own right, but rather with a transitional view . . . The view that Jesus hid his teaching by parables is however in this regard an exception . . . A further history also belongs to the idea that the resurrection separates two times in the disciples' knowledge.[7]

It is here odd that the temporal ingredient, the dénouement at Easter, that Wrede considered inherent in the total theory, but thought was so exclusively tied to the silencings rather than the parables in Mark that the silencings must be the basic ingredient in the total Messianic theory, now emerges in the subsequent history of the concept as surviving, but without the silencings, as does the parable theory. It is hence conceivable that a fuller analysis of this apparent coincidence that Wrede noted only in passing might clarify the context so lacking in Wrede's own presentation. This may be possible today not simply because of the subsequent course of Marcan-Johannine studies, but especially because of such new source material as the Nag Hammadi codices, from which some of the environment of this trajectory may be inferred. Such an investigation might also

---

[6]Wrede, *Messiasgeheimnis*, pp. 205–206 (ET, pp. 205–207).
[7]Wrede, *Messiasgeheimnis*, pp. 242–243 (ET, pp. 244–245).

draw attention to the distinctively Marcan and Johannine variant upon that context and thereby give insight into their distinctive tendency rather than (with Wrede) simply identifying it with that postulated context.

The prehistory of the Marcan chapter on parables, 4:1–34, has been worked out by Willi Marxsen.[8] To be sure, Marxsen did not then have access to the Gospel of Thomas, which presents as Saying 9 the same parable of the Sower with which Mark 4 opens, yet without any interpretation, thus suggesting a still earlier stage in the tradition than the one with which Marxsen begins. He draws attention first to the structural parallel between major segments of 4:1–20 and 7:14–23: In both cases a parable is told before a crowd, the disciples are taken aside (κατὰ μόνας/ εἰς οἶκον), and, with an identical quotation formula (καὶ λέγει αὐτοῖς), there is added an interpretation of the parable (assuming at this stage the singular both in 4:10 and 4:13). Thus, one has here an early oral stage in the transmission of the tradition,[9] once the interpretive aid of the original context in which Jesus told the parable had been lost and the need for an explicit interpretation had emerged.

The next stage is a pre-Marcan written source, imbedding the oral unit 4:3–8, 10, 13–20 into a larger whole that includes 4:3–10, 13–20, 26–32. When one takes note of the additions at this level introduced with a distinctive quotation formula καὶ ἔλεγεν 4:9, 26, 30, one catches sight of the hermeneutical nature and the direction of the tradition. Already the oral stage had to an extent reflected the hermeneutical nature of the tradition, in that the parable opened with an exhortation to hear, that is to say, to hearken at a deeper interpretive level (4:3;7:14), and the interpretation began with the pointed question: Do you not understand? (4:13;7:18). Now in the written source this is intensified at the end of the parable by the insertion of the saying: "He who has ears to hear let him hearken" (4:9). This is lacking both in the oral stage and in the Gospel of Thomas 9. In Mark 7:16 it is present only as a variant reading. Marxsen takes this as an indication that the parallel between the two chapters to

---

[8]W. Marxsen, "Redaktionsgeschichtliche Erklärung der sogenannten Parabeltheorie des Markus," *ZThK* 52 (1955): 255–71.

[9]The parallel structure in Mark 7 seems a valid basis for assuming here an oral form for appending an interpretation to a parable, rather than assuming with J. Jeremias, *Die Gleichnisse Jesu* (Göttingen[6], 1962), pp. 10–11, note 5 (Eng. tr. of the third German edition of 1954 by S. H. Hooks, *The Parables of Jesus* [New York, 1955], p. 12, note 11) that the interpretation was added in a secondary stage after the three parables had been brought together.

which he draws attention had been sensed at some time in the manuscript tradition. However it may well be that this is not the case, but rather that the saying was added here as it often was to parables or other texts calling for deeper understanding. In fact we have to do with a hermeneutical *topos*, as new source material has made abundantly clear. It occurs at the end of a parable in Matthew 13:43; Luke 14:35; Gospel of Thomas 8, 21, 63, 65, 96; Matthew 25, 29 v.l.; Luke 12:21 v.l.; 13:9 v.l.; 21:4 v.l.; Justin, Dialogue 51.3 quoting Matthew 11:15; the Naassene Hymn, Hippolytus Ref. V. 8.29, quoting Mark 4:9; and the Docetists, Hippolytus Ref. VIII, 9.1, quoting Mark 4:9. The same *topos* occurs with a comparably obscure saying of the Lord calling for interpretation, at its conclusion, in Matthew 11:15; Rev. 2:7, 11, 17, 29; 3:6, 13, 22; Gospel of Mary, P. Berol. 8502, 7:8–9; 8:10–11; Sophia of Jesus Christ, NH III, 97:20–22; 98:21–22; Pistis Sophia 17;43; or at its beginning, in the Gospel of Thomas 24; Sophia of Jesus Christ, NH III, 105:9–11; P. Berol. 8502, 107:18–108:1. In many of these instances one can on the basis of parallel texts observe the *topos* being secondarily added, for example, Matthew 25:29; Mark 7:16; Luke 12:21; 13:9; 14:35; 21:4; the Gospel of Thomas 8, 21, 63, 65, 96; the Christianized Sophia of Jesus Christ when compared with its non-Christian *Vorlage* Eugnostos the Blessed. Thus it is a floating hermeneutical *topos*, whose meaning is made clear at several occurrences. In the Gospel of Thomas 24 it is quoted and then an explanation is added: "There is light within a man of light, and he (or: it) lights up the whole world. If he (or: it) does not shine, he (or: it) is darkness."Hippolytus, Ref. VIII.9.1, citing the Docetists, quotes Mark 4:9 and adds, "since these things are not (fit) hearing for all." The *topos* occurs *passim* in Pistis Sophia, and is interpreted in Chapter 18 by Mary as being said "so that we may understand the word which thou has spoken . . . so that thou shouldest know whose heart is directed towards the Kingdom of Heaven" (see also Pistis Sophia 42 quoted below).

The written source used by Mark also included two further parables, the Seed Growing Secretly (4:26–29) and the Mustard Seed (4:30–32). Thus the parable of the Sower becomes the first parable in a series. In fact it is the basic hermeneutical parable upon which the collection is built. This is not simply indicated by the facts that it is put in first place and alone is accompanied by an explicit interpretation. Rather, the content of the interpretation is oriented in a basic way to the hermeneutical issue of how the message (λόγος) is received. This scope of this first parable recurs in the conclusion to the collection of parables in 4:33: "With many such parables he spoke the word to them" (καὶ τοιαύταις παραβολαῖς πολλαῖς ἐλάλει αὐτοῖς τὸν λόγον). The function of the interpretation is thus in a sense to explicate the *topos* we have just discussed. The basic function of the first parable with its interpretation in the collection is comparable to that of the first saying of the Gospel of Thomas (Nag Hammadi II,2; P. Oxy. 654), "Whoever finds the interpretation of these sayings will not experience death." Johannes Leipoldt[10] was so emphatic that this saying belongs to the introduction, to set the hermeneutical tone of a need for deeper understanding, that he ascribed it to Thomas rather than to Jesus. But it seems to be that in both cases one chose as the first of Jesus' sayings a saying that would serve as a hermeneutical basis for the collection to follow. This is made explicit by an insertion (Mark 4:13c) at the beginning of the hermeneutically oriented interpretation, emphasizing the first parable's foundational role for the whole collection, "Do you not understand this parable? How then will you understand all the parables?" (καὶ πῶς πάσας τὰς παραβολὰς γνώσεσθε).

The collection of parables concludes with a motif inherent in the whole hermeneutical tradition, 4:34b: "But privately to his own disciples he explained everything" (κατ᾽ ἰδίαν δὲ τοῖς ἰδίοις μαθηταῖς ἐπέλυεν πάντα). The term "privately" (κατ᾽ ἰδίαν) is in fact interchangeable with the term in 4:10 "alone" (κατὰ μόνας), and provides the historicizing framework for the interpretation. It is striking that much of this same hermeneutical mechanism recurs in Gnosticism. Irenaeus I.25.5: "Jesus, they say, spoke in a mystery to his disciples and apostles privately" (τὸν Ἰησοῦν λέγοντες ἐν μυστηρίῳ τοῖς μαθηταῖς αὐτοῦ καὶ ἀποστόλοις κατ᾽ ἰδίαν λελαληκέναι); II.27.2: ". . . they themselves testify, when they maintain that the Savior privately taught these same things not to all, but to certain only of His disciples who could comprehend them, and who understood what was intended by Him through means of arguments, enigmas, and parables" ("et ipsi testantur dicentes, in absconso haec eadem Salvatorem docuisse non omnes, sed aliquos discipulorum, qui possunt capere, et per argumenta, et aenigmata, et parabolas ab eo significata intelligentibus"). Though put within a tripartite framework, the same mechanism is discernible in the Extracts from Theo-

[10]J. Leipoldt, *Das Evangelium nach Thomas koptisch und deutsch*, TU 101, Berlin 1967, p. 7.

dotus 66: "The Savior taught the apostles, first in a figurative and mystical way, then in parables and riddles, and thirdly, clearly and directly in private" (ὁ σωτὴρ τοὺς ἀποστόλους ἐδίδασκεν, τὰ μὲν πρῶτα τυπικῶς καὶ μυστικῶς, τὰ δὲ ὕστερα παραβολικῶς καὶ ἠνιγμένως, τὰ δὲ τρίτα σαφῶς καὶ γυμνῶς κατὰ μόνας). A further *terminus technicus* is the verb ἐπιλύειν, to "resolve" the parable. Hermas, Similitudes V.5.1 ἐπιλύσεις τῶν παραβολῶν (cf. also V.3.1–2; V.4.2–3; IX.11.9); Irenaeus II.27 "absolutiones parabolarum." It occurs *passim* in Pistis Sophia that a disciple presents a "resolution." Its intimate relation to the other hermeneutical *topoi* is evident, for example, from Pistis Sophia 42: "He who has ears to hear, let him hear. And he whose Spirit wells up within him, let him come forward and say the interpretation of the thought of the fifth repentance of Pistis Sophia." This term is in fact equivalent to the term *pesher* occurring between the text and its interpretation in Qumran Pesharim, the term διδαχή occurring between the text and its interpretation in Didache 1.3, and the term ἑρμηνεία in the Gospel of Thomas 1. These terms tend to flow together in the Manichaean Kephalaia 16:35–36; 17:10–11 (chapter 2): "The first parable (παραβολή) about which they asked him and that they asked [him] to interpret (ἑρμηνεύειν) for them is this . . . (The parable "By Their Fruits" Luke 6:43–44) [We] ask you now that you [teach us concerning these] two trees [and] interpret (ἑρμηνεύειν) them [to us]." How widespread and persistent this usage was may be illustrated from the Life of Pachomius (fourth century A.D.; Vita Prima 122): "He [Horsiesios] did not only speak to them in parable (διὰ παραβολῶν), but he also gave the interpretation (σύγκρισις) of the sayings."

Although it is uncertain in some cases whether the redactional material in 4:33–34 is to be attributed to the written source or to Mark, one segment of this material seems clearly Marcan. This is the broadening of the meaning of παραβολή so that it designates the whole of Jesus' public teaching, Mark 4:34a: "He did not speak to them without a parable" (χωρὶς δὲ παραβολῆς οὐχ ἐλάλει αὐτοῖς). For the other distinctively Marcan additions, introduced with a still third form of quotation formula ἔλεγεν αὐτοῖς, reflect this view. In the presentation of the distinctively Marcan parable theory 4:11–12, "Everything is in parables" (ἐν παραβολαῖς τὰ πάντα γίνεται), the term παραβολή does not mean what we, following Jülicher, mean by parable, namely a simple sermon illustration, but rather *mashal*, puzzle, riddle, conundrum. Jesus' whole message is such a "mystery" (μυστήριον, 4:11), whose key must be "given" to the insiders. Thus the hermeneutical exhortation "He who has ears to hear let him hearken" becomes the fate-laden "though hearing they do not hearken and do not understand" of Is. 6:9–10 (Mark 4:12; cf. the Apocryphon of John, NH II, 22:26–28). This is also the gist of the two Marcan additions 4:21–23,24–25. Both are introduced with the Marcan quotation formula, and the one ends "If anyone has ears to hear let him hearken" while the other begins "See to what you hear." These sayings, themselves conundrums, convey the Marcan view: The object of the hermeneutical enterprise is what is "hid," "secret" (τι κρυπτόν, ἀπόκρυφον), which is destined to "come to light" (εἰς φανερόν, 4:22). The fate-ladenness of the hermeneutical transaction consists in the fact that the key is "given" to him who "has" (4:24). One may compare Barnabas 17:2: "You will not understand because they are hid in parables" (οὐ μὴ νοήσατε διὰ τὸ ἐν παραβολαῖς κεῖσθαι). Thus what began as a collection of sermon illustrations has become a chain of riddles. It has in substance gone through the same trajectory as did the sapiential genre of "sayings of the sages" (λόγοι σοφῶν) to end up as "secret sayings" (λόγοι ἀπόκρυφοι), by which term the Gospel of Thomas and the Book of Thomas the Contender (NH II,7) are designated in their *incipit*. [11] In fact, παραβολαί and λόγοι ἀπόκρυφοι have become synonyms and the two *genres* are one. Joachim Jeremias may be correct in pointing out that 4:21–25 is intended "as an actual double parable, and not as a collection of sayings, as is shown by the twice repeated warning to take heed in v. 23 (cf. with v. 9) and v. 24a (cf. with v. 3a),"[12] if by "collection of sayings" one has in view Q, but not if one were to think of The Gospel of Thomas, where incidentally much of this material recurs: Mark 4:3–8 cf. GTh 9; Mark 4:21 cf. GTh 33; Mark 4:22 cf. GTh 5—6; Mark 4:25 cf. GTh 21; Mark 4:29 cf. GTh 21; Mark 4:30–32 cf. GTh 20. The immediate canonical precursor to the Gospel of Thomas is thus less Q than Mark 4:1–33!

---

[11]See my article, "Logoi Sophōn: Zur Gattung der Spruchquelle Q," *Zeit und Geschichte. Dankesgabe an Rudolf Bultmann zum 80. Geburtstag*, ed. E. Dinkler (Tübingen, 1964), pp. 77–96, enlarged, revised and translated as "Logoi Sophōn: On the Gattung of Q," in *The Future of Our Religious Past. Essays in Honour of Rudolf Bultmann*, ed. J. M. Robinson (London, Evanston and New York, 1971), pp. 84–134, and in *Entwicklungslinien durch die Welt des frühen Christentums* (Tübingen, 1971), pp. 67–106 and *Trajectories Through Early Christianity* (Philadelphia, 1971), pp. 71–113.

[12]Jeremias, *Die Gleichnisse Jesu*, p. 90 (Eng. tr. p. 71).

Now this whole hermeneutical vocabulary as well as the meaning of παραβολή as conundrum is hardly an ad hoc creation that first emerged within the process of interpreting Jesus' parables. Rather, it is indicative of the context in which that process took place—the broader hermeneutical undertaking of Late Antiquity, especially that taking place within Judaism and primitive Christianity. In fact Old Testament texts can be designated parabolic, that is, enigmatic, to indicate the validity of a deeper interpretation, for example, Justin, Dialogue 52.1: "And for this reason the Holy Spirit had uttered these truths in a parable, and obscurely" (ἐν παραβολῇ δὲ καὶ παρακεκαλυμμένως τὸ πνεῦμα τὸ ἅγιον διὰ τοῦτο αὐτά ἐλελαλήκει); The Ascension (Martyrdom) of Isaiah 4:20: "And the rest of the vision of the Lord, behold, it is recorded in parables in my words which are written in the book which I openly proclaimed." Cf. also Barnabas 6.10; Pistis Sophia 18. Thus a "resolution" of an Old Testament text can be given, Pistis Sophia 63. That is to say, the Old Testament is subsequently to be decoded in a specific, for example, Christian, way: Justin, Dialogue 68.6: "There are many sayings written obscurely, or parabolically, or mysteriously, and symbolical actions, which the prophets who lived after the persons who said or did them expounded" (πολλοὺς λόγους, τοὺς ἐπικεκαλυμμένως καὶ ἐν παραβολαῖς ἢ μυστηρίοις ἢ ἐν συμβόλοις ἔργων λελεγμένους, οἱ μετ᾿ ἐκείνους τοὺς εἰπόντας ἢ πράξαντας γενόμενοι προφῆται ἐξηγήσαντο). In this context there tends also to be a time differential, as when in the Habakkuk Pesher from Qumran (to Hab. 2:2) the view is presented that Habakkuk wrote hidden meanings only divulged in the eschatological time of the Essenes. In view of the Primitive Christian understanding of Easter as the ultimate unveiling of Jesus' true role, it is not surprising that the time differential for the christological interpretation of scripture would be placed at this juncture. Thus Luke 24:25–27, 32 (cf. John 20:9) presents Jesus introducing an *interpretatio christiana* of the Old Testament at a resurrection appearance.

It would be natural that this hermeneutical plus for the time of interpretation over the time of the text, when placed by Christians at Easter, would also be applied to the tradition of Jesus' sayings as the text. The Letter of Peter to Philip (NH VIII,2) seems in this way to seek to validate the Gnostic teaching as the deeper meaning of Jesus' teaching before his death. The resurrected appears to them on "'the Mount of Olives,' the place where they used to gather with the blessed Christ when he was in the body" (VIII, 133:15–17). What he has to say is nothing new—it is the understanding of it that is new: "It is you yourselves who are witnesses that I spoke all these things to you. But because of your unbelief I shall speak again" (135:5–8); ". . . as I already [said to] you when I was in the body" (138:2–3); "I have told you many times" (138:22–24). The Apocalypse of Peter (NH VII,*3*) also presents Jesus referring back to what he had said prior to his death (72:10–13): "Peter, I have told you many times that they are blind ones who have no guide."

At times the post-Easter time of interpretation can be applied specifically to parables. In the Apocryphon of James (NH I,*2*) it is put into relation with the Gnostic motif of a final appearance 18 months after Jesus' death (7:35–8:10):

> Since I have already been glorified in this fashion, why do you hold me back in my eagerness to go? For after the [end] you have compelled me to stay with you another eighteen days (to be amended to: months?) for the sake of the parables. It was enough for some <to listen> to the teaching and understand "The Shepherd" and "The Seed" and "The Building" and "The Lamps of the Virgins" and "The Wage of the Workmen" and "The Didrachmae" and "The Woman."

An instance of such a post-Easter interpretation of a parable known from Mark 4:25; GTh 41 is provided by the Apocalypse of Peter (NH VII, 83:27—84:6):

> Therefore I said, "Everyone who has, it will be given to him, and he will have plenty. But he who does not have,"—that is, the man of this place, who is completely dead, who is removed from the planting of the creation of what is begotten, whom, if one of the immortal essence appears, they think that they possess him—"it will be taken from him" and be added to the one who is.

One way, however, in which the post-Easter time of interpretation can be set over against the time before Jesus' death is by the metaphorical or generalizing use of the term παραβολή to refer to Jesus' teaching before his death as all coded, over against which stands the uncoded (παρρησία) meaning. Wrede could in this connection refer in general to Pistis Sophia on the basis of Harnack's report. Some specific instances: Pistis Sophia 6:

> Then Jesus, the Compassionate, said to them: "Rejoice and be glad from this hour because I have been to the places from whence I came forth. From today onwards I will speak with you openly (παρρησία) from the beginning

of the truth until its completion. And I will speak with you face to face, without parable (παραβολή). I will not conceal from you, from this hour onwards, anything of the things of the height and place of the truth."

Pistis Sophia 25:

Now indeed I will not conceal anything from you from this hour, but I will reveal everything to you certainly and openly (παρρησία).

Here the coordinated pair of terms παραβολή/παρρησία emerges. Though they are not used throughout, the same position recurs, for example, Pistis Sophia 88,90,100. But with Pistis Sophia Wrede's presentation ends, on a somewhat whimsical note:

The old view of the puzzling nature of Jesus' preaching also lived on forcefully after the Gospels. No matter how much later Pistis Sophia may have originated than the Fourth Gospel, it is difficult to believe that these ideas were picked up again at a given time only as a result of reading this Gospel; rather they must have been preserved in living tradition when Gnosticism in its way took control of them.[13]

Now a text nearer in time to the Gospel of John than to Pistis Sophia fills in a part of this void in the documentation, just as it did in the case of the interpretation of parables after Easter: the Apocryphon of James (NH I,7:1–7): "At first I spoke to you in parables (παραβολή) and you did not understand; now I speak to you openly, and you (still) do not perceive."

In view of the fact that Wrede had neither analyzed the hermeneutical layers behind Mark 4 nor the then inaccessible source material subsequent to John, it is not surprising that he did not in every regard adequately identify the position on the trajectory of Mark and John and define their relations to each other. Had he recognized the extent to which the final redactional stage in Mark, in distinction from earlier layers imbedded in chapter 4, uses παραβολή to designate not just parables but Jesus' teaching as enigmatic, he would have found Mark and John even closer than he had assumed (incidentally John conversely attests the earlier layer, when παροιμία means an individual parable, 10:6). Had Wrede been able to fill out the hermeneutical trajectory more fully, he might have built primarily on the parables rather than on the silencings in order to understand the historical process. This in turn might have led him to a different

[13]Wrede, *Messiasgeheimnis*, p. 250, (ET, p. 251).

assessment of the temporal turning point in Mark and John which he identified at the resurrection, on the uncritical assumption that they conformed to the widespread Christian as well as subsequent Gnostic emphasis upon Easter as the point of revelation par excellence, a view Wrede then documented for Mark in 9:9: "And as they were coming down the mountain, he charged them to tell no one what they had seen, until the Son of man should have risen from the dead" (καὶ καταβαινόντων αὐτῶν ἐκ τοῦ ὄρους διεστείλατο αὐτοῖς ἵνα μηδενὶ ἃ εἶδεν διηγήσωνται, εἰ μὴ ὅταν ὁ υἱὸς τοῦ ἀνθρώπου ἐκ νεκρῶν ἀναστῇ).

As a consequence, Wrede relegated to insignificance the striking fact that both Mark and John make use of the pair of technical terms παρα-βολή (παροιμία) παρρησία. In the case of John he is able to relate this usage to Pistis Sophia, using it to distinguish between Jesus' teaching prior to his death, and the teaching of the resurrected, even though the relevant passage in John is placed before Jesus' death at 16:25–29. For the typically Johannine pattern of referring to the exaltation or glorification as future, but then, in the parting discourse (17:1), announcing that the hour has come, recurs also in the case of 16:25 and 16:29. Of course, even in John it would have been clearer if the shift had been marked at a resurrection appearance, which would be for John a ready possibility, since John 20 has resurrection appearances, whereas for Mark, which lacks resurrection appearances, it would not. But rather than taking the actual location of the turning point in John more seriously and facing the whole question of why the parting discourses, with their ultimacy of Johannine interpretation, precede Jesus' death, thus leaving the resurrection appearances by comparison rather conventional, Wrede accepts John 16:25–29 as the equivalent to the turning point at Easter. As a result he overlooks the comparable but even earlier Marcan text, 8:32: "And he said this plainly" (καὶ παρρησίᾳ τὸν λόγον ἐλάλει), which is in fact the redactional pendant to Mark 4:34a: "He did not speak to them without a parable" (χωρὶς δὲ παραβολῆς οὐκ ἐλάλει αὐτοῖς). To Mark 8:32 Wrede can only state:[14]

> He speaks (what is secret) openly. One need not at all think of an antithesis to earlier veiled speech, to which nothing points.

Wrede had in fact overlooked the pointer imbedded in the text!

In the Marcan context of chapter 8 the feeding of the multitude is

[14]Wrede, *Messiasgeheimnis*, p. 100 (ET, p. 100).

elevated to parabolic significance in the discussion with the disciples in the boat, where the surprised question whether they do not understand (8:17,21), the fate-laden prevention of their understanding (8:17–18), the symbolic miracle story of the blind man regaining (in)sight in a two-stage process, the prediction of the passion (at which juncture the shift to speaking παρρησία is stated), followed by the sermon on taking up one's cross, all point toward a basic shift from enigmatic to open teaching. Here Julius Wellhausen, while agreeing with Wrede that what is at issue is Mark's literary composition rather than a turning-point in Jesus' life, sees more clearly the Marcan intention:

> Peter's confession designates in Mark's view an epoch . . . With Peter's confession there begins in Mark a distinctive section (8:27—ch. 10) preparing the passion, distinguished from the earlier and from the following context by its stance . . . Hence in Mark the gospel appears imbedded in the nest between Peter's confession and the passion.[15]

That is to say, there seems to be in Mark an effort to push back the hermeneutical turning point from Easter to the point in the public ministry when Jesus began to teach kerygmatically. There are other indications in Mark, for example, the transfiguration, that Easter material is imbedded back into the public ministry. It may be that we have to do here with what was in substance the rationale for the *genre* Gospel, as an emergent orthodoxy sought to validate Jesus prior to his death as a source of ultimate interpretation, and not just as what emergent Gnosticism could all-too-readily dispense with, a coded text.

Access to the Nag Hammadi codices is only now complete. Thus far their publication has absorbed most of the energies of those specializing in this field of study. But once they have become readily accessible, a significant interpretive phase should emerge, of which the present assessment is only a premature symbol. The Nag Hammadi codices are neither the "most important" manuscript discovery, nor will their interpretation overthrow "the scholars." As a corrective of such self-serving sensationalism one may quote Claus-Hunno Hunzinger concerning the parables in the Gospel of Thomas:

> In the process the modern critical research on the Synoptics is confirmed in a fascinating way: The existence of the *genre* of sayings collections postulated by literary criticism is now demonstrated; the small isolated units transmitted

[15]J. Wellhausen, *Einleitung in die drei ersten Evangelien* (Berlin, 1905), pp. 79, 82.

without framework or situation that form criticism postulated stand here before us in just this form; the secondary elements of a predominantly allegorical or moralizing nature detected especially in the analysis of the parables as secondary (especially also the generalizing conclusions of the parables) are almost completely absent from the Gospel of Thomas.[16]

Actually the Nag Hammadi codices may do no more than vindicate the validity of intuitive insights of great minds at the opening of the century, who, without the documentation available to us, thought more deeply than have we. What they might have done, had they had at their disposal the Coptic material that has become accessible in our century! There, rather than in any presumptuous surpassing of their sparsely-documented but at times all the more brilliant hypotheses, lies a very sobering thought for New Testament scholarship to the end of the century.

[16]C.-H. Hunzinger, "Aussersynoptisches Traditionsgut im Thomas-Evangelium," *ThLZ* 85 (1960):844–46.

# LIST OF ABBREVIATIONS TO PART TWO

| | |
|---|---|
| BJRL | *Bulletin of the John Rylands Library* |
| ET | *Expository Times* |
| HNT | *Handbuch zum Neuen Testament* |
| JBL | *Journal of Biblical Literature* |
| JBR | *Journal of Bible and Religion* |
| JTS, n.s. | *Journal of Theological Studies,* new series |
| MEYER | *Kritisch-Exegetischer Kommentar über das Neue Testament,* begründet von H. A. W. Meyer |
| NTD | *Neues Testament Deutsch* |
| SJT | *Scottish Journal of Theology* |
| Str-B | Strack-Billerbeck, *Kommentar zum Neuen Testament aus Talmud und Midrasch* |
| TB | *Theologische Blätter* |
| TLZ | *Theologische Literaturzeitung* |
| TR, n.F. | *Theologische Rundschau,* neue Folge |
| TSK | *Theologische Studien und Kritiken* |
| TWNT | *Theologisches Wörterbuch zum Neuen Testament* ed. by G. Kittel and G. Friedrich |
| ZNW | *Zeitschrift für neutestamentliche Wissenschaft* |
| ZST | *Zeitschrift für systematische Theologie* |
| ZTK | *Zeitschrift für Theologie und Kirche* |

PART TWO

# The Problem of History in Mark

## III

# THE PROBLEM OF HISTORY IN THE INTERPRETATION OF MARK

A. THE NINETEENTH CENTURY: MARK AS IMMANENT, OBJECTIVE HISTORY

The traditional view of Mark as an abridgement of Matthew is responsible for the general neglect of Mark throughout the ages. But once the priority of Mark had become apparent,[1] interest in the historical Jesus rapidly directed attention to Mark. Since the earliest record is nearest the events themselves, it is most likely to have access to reliable sources (Papias pointed to Peter), and to be free from subsequent interpretation, legend-building and allegorizing (contrast John). Furthermore one proof of Marcan priority consisted in evidence that Matthew and Luke reworded Marcan stories, so that the literary personalities and theological biases of Matthew and Luke became apparent. Since there was no earlier source with which Mark could be compared, the illusion of a Marcan simplicity, neutrality, and objective historicity arose. Thus literary criticism pointed the way for the first period in Marcan interpretation.

The literary question of the interrelations among the synoptic Gospels was overshadowed by the historical issue posed by David Friedrich Strauss' *Leben Jesu* in 1835. It became necessary to prove the historicity of Jesus. The various implications of the Marcan priority for its objective historicity now came into conscious consideration, and the 'Marcan hypothesis' entered into general acceptance as a combination

[1]The first evidence that Matthew uses Mark was supplied by Christian Gottlieb Wilke in 1826 in an article 'Über die Parabel von den Arbeitern im Weinberge Matth. 20.1–16', in Winer's *Zeitschrift für wissenschaftliche Theologie*, I, 73–88. The basic argument from order, to the effect that Matthew and Luke follow the same order only when parallel to Mark, was provided by Carl Lachmann, 'De ordine narrationum in evangeliis synopticis', *SK*, VIII (1835), 570–90. Further proof from a detailed analysis of form was provided by Wilke in *Der Urevangelist*, 1838.

of two motifs: Marcan priority and Marcan objective historicity.[1] The desired reconstruction of the historical Jesus in terms of character development, psychological comprehensibility, and 'historical probability' found in Mark its documentary proof; and Mark found, through identification with this reconstruction, the proof of its objective historical character.[2]

The general assumption at the end of the nineteenth century as to Mark's understanding of history was to the effect that Mark regarded history as a series of objective events in an empirical relationship of cause and effect. The various aspects of the Marcan narrative which do not fit such a pattern can be disregarded as due to the fact that Mark was not yet a thoroughly enlightened man. The few theological (Pauline) influences can be easily identified and discounted. Such non-historical vestiges do not point toward a completely different understanding of history; they are not the points which provide the key to the whole. Rather the Marcan history is immanent and understandable in its presuppositions and intentions. Therefore a critical sifting and purification of the record does not eliminate any of the truth of history, but rather rescues what truth is present in Mark's history.

Upon this secular definition of the truth of history there was superimposed a religious, Ritschlian definition: the truth of history consists in the moral truths revealed through the teachings and examples of great men. Thus Jesus' teachings are of higher value than his action. His action is to be correlated with truth by finding in it motives or intentions which can be translated into moral principles or objectives. History has meaning as the laboratory in which truth is discovered; once the truth has been grasped and communicated to posterity, the history itself ceases to be of decisive importance. Mark tells Jesus' story to propagate the truths he learned from Jesus.

[1]This pattern was initiated by Christian Hermann Weisse, *Die Evangelische Geschichte kritisch und philosophisch bearbeitet,* 1838, and dominated the interpretation of Mark down to Heinrich Julius Holtzmann. Holtzmann provided in *Die synoptischen Evangelien,* 1863, both the most masterly proof of the priority of Mark and the most successful presentation of the historical Jesus, thus apparently proving the case for the objective historical accuracy of Mark.

[2]For the many Ritschlian lives of Jesus which are but variants of Holtzmann's synthesis, cf. Schweitzer, *The Quest of the Historical Jesus,* 193 ff. For the persistence of this approach into the following period cf. Ebeling, *Das Messiasgeheimnis und die Botschaft des Marcus-Evangelisten,* 19 ff.

## B. THE TURN OF THE CENTURY: MARK AS NON-HISTORICAL THEOLOGY

A new tack in the interpretation of Mark was inaugurated[1] by the appearance in 1901 of Wrede's *Das Messiasgeheimnis in den Evangelien.* The basic insight of Wrede is that Mark is not a transparent medium through which the historical Jesus can be easily seen. Rather Mark is a prism which must be analysed in and of itself, before conclusions can be drawn as to the historicity of what is recounted. Only by discounting the point of view and prejudice of the author can the objective historian hope to establish the real facts of Jesus' life lying behind the Marcan narrative. Wrede observed that the historical and psychological reasoning which was generally assumed to characterize Mark had in reality been read into the text. The nineteenth century had superimposed its understanding of history upon Mark.

The viewpoint of Albert Schweitzer[2] was both an alternative to and a confirmation of the position of Wrede. Schweitzer agreed with Wrede that the Marcan narrative is not built upon historical considerations of a psychological, pragmatic nature. But instead of attributing this departure from normal history to the evangelist, Schweitzer attributed it to Jesus himself. Jesus was neither psychologically predictable nor pragmatically motivated, but rather was under the sway of a dogmatic, eschatological compulsion, and consequently lived a very unusual and unlikely life. Thus, by destroying the simple, understandable Jesus, Schweitzer implicitly weakened the case for the historicizing interpretation of the Gospels which he himself employed. For by tracing the eschatological element of the narrative back to Jesus himself, he eliminated from the history of early Christianity the necessity for any period when Jesus was 'still' looked upon from an objective, immanent point of view.

Further impetus in the new orientation was provided by Wellhausen's *Einleitung in die drei ersten Evangelien,* 1905. Wellhausen works

---

[1]Already in 1892 Martin Kähler had presented in *Der sogenannte historische Jesus und der geschichtliche, biblische Christus* the view that scholarship cannot get behind the Gospels to the 'historical Jesus', since the Gospels are not historical 'sources', but rather *kerygmatic* 'witnesses'. But Kähler's influence was felt only later.

[2]Expressed first in 1901 in *The Mystery of the Kingdom of God,* then in 1906 in *The Quest of the Historical Jesus* (esp. 328 ff.).

in general independence of Wrede and Schweitzer, and yet his conclusions tend to strengthen their consensus, as well as to point the new orientation in the direction of form criticism.[1] He clearly says of Mark (43) that 'the characteristics of real historiography [*Historie*] are lacking'. Mark does not write *de vita et moribus Jesus*. He does not intend to make Jesus' person comprehensible; rather Jesus' person has been taken up and dissolved (*aufgegangen*) in his divine calling, for Mark desires to present Jesus as the Christ (44). Mark's Gospel does not give the impression of being based on the reports of Jesus' intimates; instead, long circulation as oral tradition has given the material an 'uncomfortably drastic formation' (45). In one section of Mark, between Peter's confession and Passion week, there occurs a time shift from the life of Jesus to the life of the Church; here we are confronted with what is spoken by 'the Christ to Christians' (72). This section does not supply information as to the historical Jesus; rather: 'All these things are noteworthy signs of the times in which he [sc. the Marcan Jesus] places himself', i.e., the time of the Church (70–72). Mark is thus a combination of 'memoirs and gospel' (167).

## C. RESULTANT CONFUSION: MARK AS MYTHOLOGY

The new tack in the interpretation of Mark rejected so completely the accepted canons of Marcan interpretation that the way stood open for a series of unlikely hypotheses, whose primary strength lay in the fact that they did not historicize Mark. W. Erbt, *Das Markusevangelium*, 1911, presented an interpretation of Mark in terms of astral mythology. In 1921 Arthur Drews renewed his attack upon the historicity of Jesus with a monograph *Das Markusevangelium als Zeugnis gegen die Geschichtlichkeit Jesu*, in which he drew attention to the 'mythological' point of view from which Mark was written. Old Babylonian traditions, together with astrological speculations, had been taken over by Jewish gnostics to construct a concept of a dying and rising Messiah. A similar interpretation was offered in 1924 by Hermann Raschke, *Die Werkstatt des Markusevangelisten*. The Marcan stories are but allegories of proper names venerated by the nascent religion. Raschke sees Mark as

[1] Cf., e.g., 45 of Wellhausen's work. (Citation is according to the second edition of 1911.) Cf. also Bultmann's evaluation of Wellhausen in 'The New Approach to the Synoptic Problem', *The Journal of Religion*, VI (1926), 341.

dominated by docetic and gnostic points of view, so that he arrives at the conclusion that Mark is the Gospel created by Marcion.

A scarcely needed refutation of the theses of these works was partially provided, more by coincidence than intention, by the publication in 1923 of Martin Werner's *Der Einfluss paulinischer Theologie im Markusevangelium.* This study was devoted to the disproof of any specific Pauline influence in Mark. Such an influence had been largely assumed on the basis of Gustav Volkmar's *Die Evangelien oder Marcus und die Synopsis der kanonischen und ausserkanonischen Evangelien,* 1870. Werner showed that the assumed Paulinisms of Mark were doctrines widespread in early Christianity, while the specific Pauline concepts are largely lacking in Mark. Furthermore he displayed the inadequacies of Volkmar's symbolic and allegorical interpretations, which had provided the basis for the hypotheses of the mythological school. Thus Werner closed the door through which the anti-historical Marcan interpretation was moving into gnosticism, docetism, and mysticism.

The popularization of Wrede's thesis in England[1] by R. H. Lightfoot in *History and Interpretation in the Gospels,* the Bampton Lectures of 1934, has produced a similar group of unsuccessful attempts to achieve a positive centre from which to interpret Mark. Lightfoot himself shifted his centre of interpretation a few years later[2] from the messianic secret to Lohmeyer's geographic orientation.[3] This view has found some limited acceptance, but it suffers from inner contradictions and a lack of sufficient evidence.[4] Original Anglo-Saxon presentations based upon the new orientation are to be found in Philip Carrington's *The Primitive*

[1]Lightfoot's rôle in England as a transmitter of German research has been filled in America by Frederick C. Grant, who presents in *The Earliest Gospel,* 1943, the theses, e.g., of Wrede, Werner and Lohmeyer. The ground had been prepared for Lightfoot's and Grant's monographs by A. E. J. Rawlinson's Westminster Commentary of 1925.

[2]In *Locality and Doctrine in the Gospels.*

[3]Presented in *Galiläa und Jerusalem,* 1936.

[4]Cf. the limited acceptance of W. G. Kümmel in his review of Lohmeyer's book, *TLZ,* LXII (1937), 304–7, repeated substantially in 'Das Urchristentum', *TR,* n.F., XVII (1948–9), 16–19, and the criticisms of Albrecht Oepke, *Das neue Gottesvolk,* 1950, 183–7, and Rudolf Bultmann, *Theology of the New Testament,* I, 52, 56 f. Lightfoot himself in his last work on Mark, *The Gospel Message of St. Mark,* 1950, orientates himself more to the problem of history (see below).

*Christian Calendar*; *a Study in the Making of the Marcan Gospel*, and Austin
Farrer's *A Study in St. Mark*, both of which appeared in 1952. Arch-
bishop Carrington presents the gnosticizing symbolism characteristic of
the German works, but within the framework of the cultic life of the
Church. This is combined with Lohmeyer's geographic theory and the
'numbers' symbolism of the German mythological treatments. Farrer
concentrates upon the latter trait, discovering complicated cycles and
epicycles hardly discernible even to the initiated eye.[1] The basic weakness of these works is the same methodological error which Wrede detected in the Marcan research of the nineteenth century: the argument
is not built upon what Mark clearly and repeatedly has to say, but upon
inferences as to the basis of the Marcan order, a subject upon which
Mark is silent.

The basic insight of the new orientation in Marcan research is that
Mark was not an objective historian, but rather wrote from the point
of view of Christian faith. This insight has proved to be ambiguous
and subject to misleading inferences. The various treatments based
upon the new orientation have seemed to understand 'Christian faith',
in reaction to the historicism of the nineteenth century, as some mystic,
cultic, gnostic religiosity, which more by accident than intention expresses its religious experience in terms of the action of a historical
personage. These eccentric monographs on Mark have failed to
recognize the basic fact that Mark finds meaning and divine action in
history, and therefore intends to be recording history.

### D. THE CONTEMPORARY TREND: MARK AS THEO-LOGICALLY UNDERSTOOD HISTORY

The most fruitful continuation of the new orientation consisted in
form criticism, which was less concerned with the viewpoints of the
Gospel authors (redactors?) than with the individual units within the
Gospels. However, the Marcan material provided the point of departure for form critical studies, so that inferences with regard to Mark
became apparent. Karl Ludwig Schmidt's investigation of the chronological and geographical framework of the Gospels[2] showed that Mark

[1] Cf. his retractions and corrections in: 'Loaves and Thousands', *JTS*, n.s.,
IV (1953), 1–14; and *St. Matthew and St. Mark*, 1954.
[2] *Der Rahmen der Geschichte Jesu*, 1919.

does not display a historian's concern for the externals of the history he is recording. On the other hand, form criticism eliminated pre-Marcan literary sources and Gospels. This accentuated Mark's rôle as 'historicizer' of material which had previously circulated in the context of the Church's life, but now appeared in the context of a presentation of Jesus.[1]

The intention of Mark to 'historicize' the oral tradition was traced to its origin in the centre of early Christian theology by Julius Schniewind.[2] The worship of the heavenly Lord is not a mystic experience separate from history, but is rather an awareness of living in a 'time of salvation', which would not be possible if the heavenly Lord had not brought that 'time' into history. The *kerygma* is the witness to the fact that the 'time of salvation' is present because the Messiah has been in history. To tell his 'history' as the inauguration of the 'time of salvation' is to witness to the present experience of the 'time of salvation'. The unity of the heavenly Lord of Mark's Church and the earthly Jesus of A.D. 30 lies in the continuity of the 'time of salvation'. The 'messianic secret' is but an expression of an understanding of history which embraces both the history of Jesus and the history of the Church. Since the Church sees its history founded in Jesus' history, it can witness to and explain its religious experience better by writing the history of Jesus as the Messiah than by describing its own religious life.

Schniewind's position is presented partially in terms of an interpretation of K. L. Schmidt's intention, and Schmidt accepts this interpretation as 'the best'.[3] Schmidt then defines the two limits between which a correct interpretation lies. One must avoid both an 'individualistic-psychological' approach, which bases itself upon a correct observation of the 'concrete-human' aspect of the Gospel narrative (Ebionitism),

---

[1]This emphasis in Martin Dibelius' *Formgeschichte des Evangeliums*, 1919, 2nd ed. 1933, is obscured in the English translation *From Tradition to Gospel*. Dibelius refers three times to Mark as 'historicizing' (*historisieren*) the material, but in only one case, p. 223, does the English translation preserve this significant term. In the other two instances it is obscured by the very free renderings: 224, 'would-be history'; 225, 'touched . . . up'.

[2]In his article 'Zur Synoptiker-Exegese', TR, n.F., II (1930), 129–89. The results of this analysis were applied in his commentaries to Mark (1933, 6th ed. 1952) and Matthew (1936, 6th ed. 1953) in the series *Das Neue Testament Deutsch*.

[3]In a lecture of 1933–4 on 'Das Christuszeugnis der synoptischen Evangelien', published in Beiheft 2 of *Evangelische Theologie*, 7–33.

and a 'collectivistic-cultic' or 'mythological' approach, which bases itself upon a correct observation of those aspects of the Gospel which cannot be grasped psychologically (Docetism). Although the synoptic Gospels are not interested in uncommitted objective narration, they do intend to narrate history. It is true that extraneous traits, such as debates in the early Church's life or Hellenistic religious motifs, are visible in the Gospel narration. Yet they are not told as the Church's religious experience or as comparative religion, but are told as part of the history of the Messiah. Therefore a 'messianic' interpretation should supersede a 'stylistic' or 'comparative religion' analysis.[1] Here Schmidt has laid bare the ambiguity involved in the simple affirmation of the new orientation that the Gospels are to be interpreted primarily as a documentation of the history of the early Church. He himself operates upon the basis of this new orientation, but proceeds to point to the fact about the history of the early Church which had been largely ignored: the early Church had a vital concern for the redemptive history of Jesus. With regard to the affirmation *Deus dixit* the particular rôle of the synoptic Gospels is to emphasize that this perfect tense, while being a present perfect, is nevertheless a perfect tense.[2]

The most significant monograph on Mark in this period is that by Hans Jürgen Ebeling, *Das Messiasgeheimnis und die Botschaft des Marcus-Evangelisten*, 1939. This work presents first a history of the problem of the messianic secret, in which the method of Wrede but not his solution is defended. The second half of the work consists in retracing Wrede's investigation of the silencing of the demons, the disciples' lack of understanding, and the parable theory. The two motifs of secrecy and misunderstanding reveal the Church's understanding of itself correlative to its understanding of Jesus. These two motifs give expression to the two sides of 'Christian faith's understanding of itself' (223). The secrecy passages accentuate the majesty of Jesus so as to convey that motif of faith which Ebeling designates 'the "must" of faith as the flow-

---

[1]Schmidt's illustration: Bultmann's interpretation of the temple-tax pericope: 'Discussions of the Palestinian Church about responsibility for the temple-tax', is less appropriate to the Gospel's intention than Calvin's: 'We must attend, first of all, to the design (scopus) of this narrative; which is, that Christ, by paying tribute of his own accord, declared his subjection, as he had taken upon him the form of a servant.'

[2]The view of Schmidt is adopted by E. Käsemann in his lecture to 'old Marburgers' in 1953, published in the *ZTK*, LI (1954), 125–53.

ing, free impulse of the heart.' Similarly the misunderstanding motif points to the revelation-character of Jesus in order to express the believer's tension and difficulty in arriving at a true understanding of himself.

Here for the first time in Marcan interpretation a concerted effort is made to characterize the religious experience of the Marcan Church as reflected in its presentation of the history of Jesus. Such an analysis is indispensable if Mark is to be seen as *kerygmatic* history in distinction from objective history. Yet the emphasis of Ebeling again jeopardizes the basic relevance of the fact that Mark presents his confession as a history not of himself but of Jesus. Ebeling does not look upon the Marcan Jesus as sufficiently concrete, real, or literal to be himself the subject of analysis and clarification. Rather each trait is immediately introverted into its existential meaning. The Marcan unity is sought in an understanding of religious experience, rather than in an understanding of Jesus as the basis of that experience. Marcan theology reflects a religious *a priori*, rather than a prior historical event. Thus Ebeling does not grasp the relationship between the history of Jesus as the inauguration of the eschatological 'time of salvation', and the existence of Mark as existence within this eschatological history. He reduces this relationship to the subjective tension in the believer's religious experience, thus neglecting the historical cast of Mark's presentation and the problem of history which it presents.[1] However it is only by defining Mark's understanding of history that a centre of interpretation can be located which does justice both to Mark's history of Jesus and to Mark's religious experience. Until this understanding of history is clarified, Marcan interpretation must fluctuate between the dissolution of the Marcan history of Jesus into Mark's religious experience, and the petrifaction of the Marcan *kerygma* into objective historiography.

### E. THE CONTEMPORARY DEBATE ABOUT HISTORY

Ever since Kierkegaard's 'infinite qualitative difference' between time and eternity was introduced as the basis for theological thought,[2] and the reaction against 'historicism' became generally prevalent in

[1]Cf. the critical reviews by Lohmeyer, *TLZ*, LXV (1940), 18–22, and by Kümmel, 'Das Messiasgeheimnis im Markusevangelium', *Kirchenblatt für die reformierte Schweiz*, XCVI (1940), 2–5.

[2]Cf. the preface to the second edition (1921) of Karl Barth's *Romans*.

theological circles,[1] the relationship of Christianity to history has been central in theological debate. It is today becoming apparent that Barth's anti-historicism of the twenties was embedded in a positive concern for the meaning of history, which had been more apparent in the first (untranslated) edition of the *Römerbrief* (1919), and which has reappeared in the more recent volumes of the *Kirchliche Dogmatik*.[2] The sharp terminological cleavage between history and God which characterized the twenties has continued into the New Testament scholarship of the present primarily in the publications of Rudolf Bultmann[3] and Ernst Fuchs.[4]

It has become customary in German theology to distinguish between history *in bonam partem* as *Geschichte*, and history *in malam partem* as *Historie*. The former refers to history as encountered existentially for the meaning it conveys, while the latter refers to history examined objectively for its mere factuality. But in Bultmann's writing *Geschichte* also tends increasingly to be used *in malam partem*, for it occurs in such associations as 'inner-historical development', 'empirical-historical', 'national history', 'this-worldly history'. This kind of history can be prophecy or 'saving history' only by failing, coming to an end, i.e., by demonstrating the futility of trusting in man and thereby pointing to God, the *eschaton*.[5] Therefore, while Bultmann can still speak of 'God's

[1] Cf. Troeltsch's *Der Historismus und seine Probleme*, 1922, and his English lectures: *Christian Thought: its History and Application*, 1923.

[2] Cf. IV. i (1953), 246–50 for his specific appropriation of the attitude toward the synoptics characteristic of Schmidt and Käsemann.

[3] Cf. especially: 'Heilsgeschichte und Geschichte', *TLZ*, LXXIII (1948), 659–66; 'Weissagung und Erfüllung', *ZTK*, XLVII (1950), 360–83; and most recently his presidential address to the *Studiorum Novi Testamenti Societas* published *NTS*, I (1954), 5–16: 'History and Eschatology in the New Testament'. In the present discussion these essays are cited according to page number only.

[4] Cf. his lecture 'Christus das Ende der Geschichte', *Evangelische Theologie*, Jahrgang 1948–9 (1949), 447–61. He defines history (457, n. 18) as 'temporally fallen Being, in which man bequeaths his efforts at being able to live, since he attempts to surpass himself.'

[5] This is the argument in 'Weissagung und Erfüllung', 380 f. Similarly in 'Heilsgeschichte und Geschichte', col. 665: 'According to primitive Christian thinking, Christ is rather *the end of history and of saving history*. The appearance of Jesus "as the time was full" (Gal. 4.4), signifies the eschatological event which places an end to the old aeon. From now on there can be no more history, and also no saving history, which precisely has reached in him its goal.' This is worked out more fully in 'History and Eschatology in the New Testament'.

deed in history',[1] he tends to give expression to the positive residue in the term 'history' by making use of two derivatives: 'saving event'[2] on the one hand and the 'historicity'[3] of human Being on the other. The former stands over against a linear, causally-connected, evolutionistic view of history, and accentuates the punctiliar, vertical aspect of the encounter with the *kerygma*. Such an encounter is 'eschatological', a term which now stands in antithesis to 'historical'.[4] The second term, 'historicity', does not characterize that which is encountered, but rather the attitude of him who enters the encounter. As such, it is a definition of 'faith', which is for Bultmann the pre-requisite to a definition of the 'ground of faith', and thus of normative Christian proclamation.[5] Both terms stand over against any objective view of history in its pastness and empiricalness, and indicate that history's meaning is apparent only as it happens and is encountered. They are also intended to avoid any group concept of history in favour of an individual relation to God, and to avoid any immanent, available and controllable relation to God.

Within the correlation between 'eschatological event' and 'historicity' is to be found the norm of Bultmann's theology.[6] The 'eschatological event' is the encounter with the message of the opportunity, the freedom,

---

[1] Weissagung und Erfüllung', 376. Cf. 'History and Eschatology in the New Testament', 16: 'The eschatological event has happened within history'.

[2] '*Heilsgeschehen*.' Cf. how this term is introduced into the article 'Heilsgeschichte und Geschichte', coll. 662ff., in working out the legitimate meaning of *Heilsgeschichte*, which term is then rejected. Similarly in the *Theology of the New Testament*, II, 121, the traditional terminology for expressing the Christian dialectic, history of salvation and world history, is replaced by the terminology 'revelation and history'. Here the term 'history' (*Geschichte!*) is reserved for the negative usage, and such an expression as 'historical revelation' becomes impossible.

[3] *Geschichtlichkeit.* Cf. 'History and Eschatology in the New Testament', 13. Is this also the German original of 'the history of man as person' (16)? A synonym is 'the temporality of Christian Being', cf. 'Heilsgeschichte und Geschichte', col. 666.

[4] This is supported by the non-historical dimensions of apocalypticism's concept of the new aeon, which for the NT—at least its normative parts—is applied to the present existence of the Christian. This thesis is worked out in the essay 'History and Eschatology in the New Testament', with the conclusion (13 and 16): 'History is swallowed up in eschatology.'

[5] 'Heilsgeschichte und Geschichte', col. 662.

[6] Such an approach provides a more direct entry into the centre of the Bultmannian theology than does the ontological dualism postulated by Heinrich Ott in his valuable study of *Geschichte und Heilsgeschichte in der Theologie Rudolf Bultmanns*, 1955.

to be found in accepting one's death. (This message is the message of 'the resurrection' or the *kerygma*.) But a message whose content was a doctrine either to be accepted without insight or to be understood as a demonstrable universal principle would provide an inner contradiction to the existential meaning of the eschatological event itself. Such a message would not lead to insight into one's historicity, but rather the contrary. For 'historicity' means an attitude built upon the acceptance of one's individual death ('dying with Christ'), and therefore directed toward the particular experiences of one's own life as the scope of ultimate meaning for the individual ('risen with Christ'). Therefore the *kerygma* must proclaim that God is encountered within one's historical existence. It is in this carefully defined context that a 'historical' encounter is for Bultmann indispensable. But such a context does not necessitate a history of Jesus. It is therefore questionable for Bultmann whether the early Christian understanding of history motivated Mark to begin the writing of Gospels, or whether the synoptic evangelists have not already forsaken the original Christian viewpoint.[1]

Bultmann's purification of the concept of history has become a norm by which the New Testament literature is classified, with a scale which runs from 'dehistoricizing' (Paul)[2] to 'historiography' (Luke).[3] In view

---

[1]The latter is suggested in vol. II of Bultmann's *Theology of the New Testament* (1955), by the rather cursory treatment of the synoptics within 'the development toward the Ancient Church', after the New Testament has reached its normative climax in John.

[2]*Entgeschichtlichung.* This identification is made and this viewpoint advocated by Bultmann in 'History and Eschatology in the New Testament', and by Fuchs in 'Christus das Ende der Geschichte'. The core of their argument (Bultmann, 132; Fuchs, 454) is based on the assumption that what Paul says of the law in Rom. 10.4, can be generalized to apply to his concept of history as well. Inconsistently enough, the term 'dehistoricizing' is also used by Bultmann *in malam partem* (*Das Urchristentum im Rahmen der antiken Religionen*, 1949, 65), to characterize Jewish legalism's neglect of responsibility for present history and its decisions, i.e., for the abandonment of its own historicity. On 87 f. the positive usage of the term is distinguished as equivalent to 'desecularizing' (*Entweltlichung*). This means the rejection of all wordly security, or of all that is at one's disposal, and the confrontation with one's neighbour and with God's claim.

[3]*Historie.* The present depreciation of Luke stems from Franz Overbeck (*Christentum und Kultur*, 1919, 80–82), who maintained the incompatibility of history and Christianity. His position was thus diametrically opposed to that of Harnack, who attempted to identify history and Christianity, and conse-

of this new 'tendency criticism', the relevance of investigating Mark's understanding of history is apparent.[1] For it is in terms of such individual analyses that the relationships within the New Testament literature, the dominant stream within the New Testament, and the validity or limitations of such constructions become visible. The present monograph does not approach Mark's understanding of history primarily with questions preformed by the current alternatives; rather the attempt is made to follow in form as well as content the Marcan material itself. But when this has been done, the relation to the current debate will be apparent.

---

quently thought well of Luke and his 'great historical work' (*Luke the Physician*, 1). Therefore the ensuing reaction against Harnack brought with it a depreciation of Luke. At the time that Overbeck's antithesis between history and Christianity was gaining acceptance through the dialectic theologians (cf. Karl Barth's 'Unerledigte Anfragen an die heutige Theologie', 1920, *Ges. Vortr.* II, 1–25), Overbeck's evaluation of Luke was cited with approval by Karl Ludwig Schmidt ('Die Stellung der Evangelien in der allgemeinen Literaturgeschichte', *Gunkel-Festschrift*, II [1923], 132): 'Nothing is more characteristic of Luke's conception of the Gospel history, in so far as he looked upon it as the object of historical narration, than his idea of giving the *Gospel* an Acts of the Apostles as its continuation. This is a tactlessness of world-historical dimensions, the greatest excess of false viewpoint which Luke committed.' Cf. more recently Ernst Käsemann, 'Das Problem des historischen Jesus', *ZTK*, LI (1954), 138; 'If the problem of historiography is in the other Gospels a sub-problem within eschatology, in Luke eschatology has become a sub-problem within historiography.' Similarly Bultmann, 'Heilsgeschichte und Geschichte', col. 665; 'History and Eschatology in the New Testament', 7: 'In the New Testament (if we set aside Luke–Acts) the Old Testament view of history is preserved as well as the apocalyptic view, but in such a way that the apocalyptic view prevails.' This classification of Luke as falling outside of the central view of primitive Christianity is worked out more fully in Bultmann's *Theology of the New Testament*, II, Paragraphs 53–54, 111 ff. This thesis with regard to Luke has been presented in detail by Hans Conzelmann, *Die Mitte der Zeit*, 1954.

1 In *Die Geschichte der synoptischen Tradition*, 2. Aufl., 1931, 374, Bultmann states that Mark is more mythical than Matthew and Luke. This same view is presented in his *Theology of the New Testament*, II, 124–6. In distinction from Matthew's Jewish pattern of prophecy and fulfilment, Mark sees Jesus' life in the Hellenistic pattern of an 'epiphany of the Son of God', so that one could speak of the *history* of Jesus only in quotation marks. Emphasizing miraculous events like the baptism and transfiguration, Mark sees in Jesus 'the miraculous manifestation of divine dealing in the cloak of earthly occurrence'. Yet Mark, by the very fact of giving his presentation 'the form of an historical presentation, a "life of Jesus",' reflects the early Christian

awareness that their revelation comes not in the pictures of ecstatic visionaries, nor by some unconfirmable myth, but 'by an historical figure, Jesus'. But Bultmann does not go on to inquire as to whether this side of the early Christian message found expression in various details within the Marcan presentation. Such an investigation is reserved for Luke, where such details are then characterized as evidence that Luke falls without the scope of primitive Christianity. Such a pattern of argumentation would be more compelling if it had been first demonstrated that such motifs were lacking in Mark.

# IV

# THE MARCAN INTRODUCTION: 1.1-13

## A. THE FRAMEWORK OF THE INTRODUCTION

Mark does not confront us as a philosopher writing about a concept of history, but as a narrator of history. His understanding of history must be deduced from the way he goes about writing it. His subject matter is 'the good news about Jesus Christ'. Yet the first verse is concerned not simply with the definition of the subject matter, but also with the location of its 'beginning'. Here Mark is using what seems to have been a technical term employed by the early Church for defining the *kerygma* (Luke 23.5; Acts 10.37) and apostleship (Luke 1.2; Acts 1.22; John 15.27). It was adopted by all the evangelists in their presentations: Matt. 4.17; Luke 3.22; 4.21; Acts 1.1; John 1.1; 2.11. In view of such a deliberate beginning, one is struck by the fact that Mark opens *in medias res*. He picks up the story of Jesus at a point in his adulthood, whereas he had at his disposal (cf. 6.3) information concerning Jesus' background which he does not here use. Yet on the other hand his point of departure is not really hasty, but somewhat leisurely: he does not even begin 'the good news about Jesus Christ' with the principal subject Jesus, but rather with John the Baptist. It is only with vv. 14-15, 'after John had been arrested', that Jesus' own ministry is introduced, summarized, and initiated. To understand Mark in his approach to history, we must first understand his deliberate point of departure. When this is clarified we will already be on the way to understand his choice of subject matter, his particular way of treating his subject matter, his reason for writing history at all, and the understanding of history which underlies the whole.

The narrative is delimited by the coming (v. 4) and going (v. 14) of John, so that the fulfilment is initiated within the framework of the ministry of John. To be sure vv. 9-13 form a transition from John to Jesus: Jesus' baptism by John and his temptation. Yet this section still belongs to the introduction orientated to John's ministry: The stylistic similarity between v. 9 (Jesus' baptism by John), and v. 5 (John's general baptism), tends to place the baptism of Jesus within the framework of John's ministry of baptism. The break at v. 14 is also more prominent stylistically than that at v. 9, since v. 14 provides a formal termination to John's ministry and a formal introduction to Jesus' ministry.[1]

Evidently two motifs are at work in Mark: a distinction of John's ministry from previous Judaism (1.1 ff.), and a distinction of Jesus' ministry from John's (1.14 ff.). Both motifs are sufficiently attested elsewhere in the New Testament to make it apparent that we have to do here with a topic of some theological importance for the early Church.[2] The former motif is attested in Acts 1.22, 'beginning from the baptism of John', for the meaning of 'beginning from . . .' seems to be: 'beginning with and including'.[3] If Acts 1.22 is thus co-ordinate with Mark 1.1 ff., then Acts 10.37, 'beginning with Galilee after the baptism which John preached', is more co-ordinate with Mark 1.14, 'after John was arrested' (so Luke 3.20 f.; cf. also Luke 23.5). Both motifs are evident in the collection of sayings about John in Matt. 11.9–14, and in Acts 13.24 f.; 19.3 f.

The impact of the early Church's concern with including or excluding John's ministry is less felt in the formation of Matthew, for here the interest in the infancy has priority. But Luke has succeeded in providing

[1]The earlier tendency to make a principal break after v. 8, as in the Westcott-Hort text still followed by Nestle, has largely given way to the view here represented. The unity of 1.1–13 has been a repeated emphasis of R. H. Lightfoot, *History and Interpretation in the Gospels*, 1935, 62 f.; *Locality and Doctrine in the Gospels*, 1938, 113 f.; *The Gospel Message of St. Mark*, 1950, 16 f. Cf. also Vincent Taylor, *The Gospel according to St. Mark*, 1952, 151; Erich Klostermann, *Das Markusevangelium* (HNT), 4. Aufl., 1950, 1; Julius Schniewind, *Das Evangelium nach Markus* (NTD), 6. Aufl., 1952, 42; Ernst Lohmeyer, *Das Evangelium des Markus* (Meyer), 11. Aufl., 1951, 9, and on 1.9–11.

[2]This observation was made in a general way as early as Carl Lachmann, 'De ordine narrationum in evangeliis synopticis', *TSK*, VIII (1835), 584: 'An primum quidem omnium evangelicarum narrationum principium dubitari non potest quin fuerit ab Iohanne baptista ductum: nam quae Mattheus et Lucas de Jesu pueritia referunt, ea satis adparet paucis narratoribus propria fuisse nec vulgo cognita.'

[3]This is the meaning of Luke 23.5; 24.47; cf. also Matt. 20.8; John 8.9 (cf. Blass-Debrunner, *Grammatik des neutestamentlichen Griechisch*, 8. Aufl., 1949–50, Par. 419, 3). Since neither Luke nor the earlier tradition presents the twelve as having been with Jesus from the baptism on, Acts 1.22 must be looked upon as evidence of some theological interest in 'beginning with John'.

an infancy narrative which maintains the temporal precedence of John within the Gospel, while in Luke 3.20 f. the ministry of John is excluded from the period of Jesus' public ministry by a *tour-de-force*. In Mark's case, the two foci of interest are presented in their simplest form. Jesus' ministry begins only 'after John was arrested' (1.14), yet the 'beginning of the good news about Jesus Christ' (1.1) is the ministry of John. Thus the ministry of John is set apart, as having a special preparatory significance for the ministry of Jesus, from Judaism on the one hand and from Jesus' ministry on the other.

It is striking that the 'beginning of the gospel' is announced in v. 1, but 'preaching the gospel' is mentioned only at the second introduction (vv. 14–15).[1] John preached a 'baptism of repentance for the remission of sins' (v. 4); Jesus preached 'the gospel' (v. 14). Are we to understand that the good news began to happen—in the baptism that John preached—before it began to be proclaimed as such?[2] This is not inherently impossible, so long as the good news is not conceived of as some abstract, non-historical truth which, by being eternal, has no beginning save the beginning equal to its discovery or proclamation.

[1]By failing to observe this second motif Hans Conzelmann, 'Zur Lukas-analyse', *ZTK*, IL (1952), 20, has set up a point of opposition between Mark and Luke which does not exist: 'only now [sc. Luke 3.19 f., i.e., after John] arises—in conscious opposition to Mark—the entity "gospel", the kingdom of God'. However it is precisely Mark who says (1.14 f.) that after John was imprisoned the gospel began to be preached and the kingdom to be announced. Furthermore Luke also has the other emphasis of including John: cf. the infancy narrative; the great significance he places upon dating accurately in terms of world history the beginning of John's ministry (but not Jesus' ministry!); and Acts 1.22 (which Conzelmann [ibid.] incorrectly harmonizes with the Lucan passages beginning *after* John).

[2]It is unlikely that Mark envisaged the content of the 'gospel' in 1.14 f. in conformity with the general early Christian 'gospel' of the cross and resurrection. This improbability is evident from Wellhausen's harmonizing attempts, *Einleitung in die drei ersten Evangelien*, 2nd. ed., 1911, 100. Recognizing that the content of the 'gospel' is here 'the time has been fulfilled and the reign of God has drawn near', he states that for the Jewish listeners the judgement is not *good* news and the future coming of the kingdom no news at all. He concludes that the allusions here to 'gospel' are 'Christian embellishments' which do not agree with the content of the gospel as here stated by Mark. Thus 'gospel' has here the same *kerygmatic* meaning as elsewhere in the early Church, at the expense of making Mark's presentation in 1.14 f. meaningless. E. G. Gulin, *Die Freude im N.T.*, 1932, I, 33, proposes the 'victories' of the inbreaking kingdom as the content of the 'gospel' in 1.14 f. But Mark has recorded only one victory: the temptation.

If the good news is basically occurrence, something which happens, then it can begin to happen before it is proclaimed to have begun.

It is further remarkable that the good news is introduced (v. 2) with a prophecy announcing what *will* happen: κατασκευάσει, whereas the good news as summarized on Jesus' lips (v. 15) consists in an announcement of what *has* happened: πεπλήρωται, ἤγγικεν. The future tense in the prophecy is normal, and is restrained by the present tense ἀποστέλλω. But the exclusive use of the perfect tense (v. 15) to announce the nearness of a future eschatological consummation is worthy of note. For even though we must understand ἤγγικεν to mean 'has drawn near' rather than 'has come',[1] it still refers to something having taken place: the times have shifted, the kingdom is now near because it has moved from a vague distance to a near position, a shift which has already taken place. When vv. 2-3 offer a prophecy, and v. 15 speaks of the 'time' having been 'fulfilled', are we not led by Mark to look in the intervening narrative (vv. 4-13) for an event of fulfilment?

## B. JOHN THE BAPTIST AS THE PROPHESIED PREPARER, 1.2-8

The fact that the ministry of John is seen from the viewpoint of fulfilment is confirmed by an analysis of the Marcan presentation of John. This presentation is characterized by a remarkable correlation of prophecy (vv. 2-3) and history (vv. 4-8).

The prophecy is not presented 'objectively' in the sense of a historical-critical exegesis of the Old Testament. Rather the prophecy is composed—by Mark or a predecessor—by uniting two separate passages, each of which stated the meaning of what has taken place: the way has been prepared; compare v. 2: κατασκευάσει τὸν ὁδόν, with

[1] The contrary view of C. H. Dodd, *The Parables of the Kingdom*, 1935, was refuted by J. Y. Campbell, 'The kingdom of God has come', *ET*, XLVIII (1936-7), 91-94. Dodd's reply, 'The kingdom of God has come', *ET*, XLVIII (1936-7), 138-42, was further refuted by K. Clark, 'Realized Eschatology', *JBL*, LIX (1940), 367-74. The debate seems to have been won by Campbell and Clark. See most recently R. H. Fuller, *The Mission and Achievement of Jesus*, (*Studies in Biblical Theology*, No. 12), 1954, 20 ff.; R. Morgenthaler, *Kommendes Reich*, 1952, 35 ff.; W. G. Kümmel, *Verheissung und Erfüllung*, 2. Aufl., 1953, 13-18. The same debate occurred a century earlier between Oldshausen (the viewpoint of Dodd) and von Hofmann, cf. *Weissagung und Erfüllung*, II (1844), 68: 'The perfect tense ἤγγικεν does not say that the heavenly kingdom is already there, but only that it is near.'

v. 3: ἑτοιμάσατε τὸν ὁδόν. What is prophesied is a next-to-the-last stage, a 'messenger' who will 'prepare', a 'voice' calling for 'preparedness'.

Similarly the historical narration (vv. 4–8) is directly concerned only with John; he for whom John is the preparation is not named. The history of John is not noticeably concerned with 'objectivity' in the sense of easily identifiable sources, fulness of detail, logical consistency, or the disinterested attempt to narrate 'as it happened to happen'. Hardly in a strictly statistical sense did 'all' (v. 5) come out to John (but cf. 11.32; Luke 7.29), nor do we feel called upon either to locate a specific 'wilderness' (v. 4) which runs along the edge of the Jordan.[1] Rather the historical narrative is formed and trimmed by Mark so as to set forth its true meaning: John is the prophesied preparer. The 'wilderness' is to be located not so much in relation to the Jordan as in relation to the third line of the prophecy.[2] 'All' come (cf. Acts 13.24) so that his 'way' may be truly prepared; for only a national repentance, not individual penitents, would constitute the anticipated preparation.[3] Such repentance was based on divine sanction, so that it was sometimes conceived of as limited to a certain period.[4] The detailed description of John in v. 6 occurs not out of 'biographical' interest, but to document the fact of the prophesied preparer's 'wilderness' life. The description of him as ἐνδεδυμένος . . . ζώνην δερματίνην περὶ τὴν ὀσφὺν αὐτοῦ has the specific purpose of implying John to be the preparer, Elijah redivivus (cf. 9.13), who is described in II Kings 1.8 as ζώνην δερματίνην περιεζωσμένος τὴν ὀσφὺν αὐτοῦ. Other information available to Mark concerning John (cf. 2.18; 11.32) is passed by as unrelated to the idea of fulfilment, while his suffering (6.14–29; 9.13) is reserved for the dividing line between John and Jesus (1.14).

One historical fact about John which was not evident in the prophecy was nevertheless too prominent to be excluded: the fact that he

---

[1]Cf. K. L. Schmidt, *Der Rahmen der Geschichte Jesu*, 21 f.

[2]The 'wilderness' is however an old part of the tradition (Matt. 11.7, 18 par.), whose historicity need not be put in question. Cf. M. Dibelius, *Die urchristliche Überlieferung von Johannes dem Täufer*, 1911, 9 ff., and C. H. Kraeling, *John the Baptist*, 1951, 10 ff.

[3]Cf. Strack-Billerbeck, *Kommentar zum Neuen Testament aus Talmud und Midrasch*, I, 162–5 to Matt. 4.17; further Lightfoot, *The Gospel Message of St. Mark*, 19.

[4]Cf. Windisch, *Der Hebräerbrief* (HNT), 2. Aufl., 1931, Exkurs zu Heb. 6.8; further Lohmeyer, 'Die Versuchung Jesu', *ZST*, XIV (1937), 645.

baptized. Yet this fact too is brought into conformity with the prophecy. The baptism is presented as something 'proclaimed', putting it into the framework of the preparatory action of a 'messenger' or of a 'voice of one crying'. This preparatory significance of John's baptism is stressed (v. 8) by stating the relationship and contrast between the ministries of John and Jesus in terms of two kinds of baptism. For apart from this interest in placing John's baptism in a correct relationship to Jesus, it is not customary for Mark to present Jesus' activity from the point of view of a kind of baptism he administered.[1] Furthermore it is those whom John has baptized who are to receive Jesus' baptism: 'I baptized you . . . but he will baptize you.' Thus in spite of the contrasts in the two baptisms, Jesus' activity is clearly built upon and even to a certain extent modelled after the baptism of John. The reality or efficacy of the preparatory work of John's baptism is demonstrated in the subsequent sub-section (vv. 9–13), where the baptism of Jesus by the Spirit (v. 10) is prepared for in his baptism by John (v. 9), and this baptism is presented in formal parallelism to John's general baptism (v. 5). The break-through which is dramatically presented in vv. 10 ff. is made along the 'way' which John's baptism has 'prepared'.

The narrative in which the fulfilment of the prophecy is presented culminates in its turn with John's prophecy (vv. 7 f.). For just as the history of John is understood as flowing out of and in accordance with the plan of God proclaimed by Isaiah, the history of Jesus is given the focus of fulfilment by the prophecy of John. John's spoken prophecy is itself a commentary, an explication of the meaning of his actions. His prophecy conforms to the same formal pattern of predecessor and successor as did that of Isaiah, save that now the primary emphasis is upon him for whom John prepares, and only the secondary emphasis upon John.

### C. THE COSMIC LANGUAGE OF THE BAPTISM AND TEMPTATION, 1.9–12

In John's prophecy we find ourselves already projected into cosmic language, and this shift in terminology is the most striking formal difference between the narrative concerning Jesus during the time of

---

[1] 10.38–39 and 1.8 are not parallel in meaning for Mark, although they could have been for John or Jesus.

John (vv. 9–13), and the narrative concerning John's own ministry (vv. 4–8). John's ministry is certainly intended as God's history, the fulfilment of prophecy, the effecting of the forgiveness of sins, the preparation of the messianic age. Yet it cannot be unintentional that in vv. 4–8 we find only John and the crowds, John baptizing and crowds repenting, whereas in vv. 9–13 (as intimated in the prophecy vv.7–8) we find the heavens splitting, the spirit descending like a dove, a voice from heaven, God's Son, the Spirit driving him into the wilderness, Satan tempting, with the wild beasts and ministering angels. The disappearance of all humans from the narrative after the act of baptism is accentuated by the address of the heavenly voice to Jesus rather than to the crowd or John. Jesus has his place in the human, historical language with which John and his followers are described, but also in the cosmic language of God versus Satan.

The specific purport of the various events following immediately upon Jesus' baptism can hardly be made clear by separate analysis of each individually. Only the total of the various motifs can provide an indication of what is intended. The language of Jewish hope was not homogeneous, nor does the fulfilment here any more than in vv. 4–8 correspond exactly to preconceived ideas. Yet the exceptional nature for Jewish thought of such events as here portrayed and their intimate eschatological associations in the Jewish tradition make it clear that together this cluster of cosmic events signifies for Mark a decisive occurrence in the realization of the eschatological hope.[1]

[1]Perhaps the most remarkable parallel to Mark's baptism and temptation narrative is the Testament of Levi 18, 5–12: 'The heavens shall exult in his days, and the earth shall be glad, and the clouds shall rejoice, and the angels of the glory of the presence of the Lord shall be glad in him. The heavens shall be opened, and from the temple of glory shall come upon him sanctification, with the Father's voice as from Abraham to Isaac. And the glory of the Most High shall be uttered over him. and the spirit of understanding and sanctification shall rest upon him. For he shall give the majesty of the Lord to His sons in truth for evermore; and there shall none succeed him for all generations for ever. And in his priesthood the gentiles shall be multiplied in knowledge upon the earth, and enlightened through the grace of the Lord: in his priesthood shall sin come to an end, and the lawless shall cease to do evil. And he shall open the gates of paradise, and shall remove the threatening sword against Adam. And he shall give to the saints to eat from the tree of life, and the spirit of holiness shall be on them. And Beliar shall be bound by him, and he shall give power to His children to tread upon the evil spirits.' Here all the cosmic language of Mark's presentation is either explicit or implicit.

The temptation narrative, just like the baptism narrative, contains various traits which serve more to point to the exceptional nature of what is happening than to give a clear interpretation of it. Of more significance than the individual traits of the temptation narrative is the fact that this narrative is combined with the baptism narrative at all. The Spirit, rather than separating Jesus from historical involvement with its ambiguity and cost, takes him directly into encounter with evil in the person of its cosmic head. Thus the shift noted above from historical to cosmic language has not entailed a shift from historical involvement to mysticism or 'otherworldliness'. It is rather the reverse, with the cosmic language only serving to accentuate the ultimate significance of the engagement. For Mark, just as for Rev. 12, the shift in the status of heaven signalling the arrival of God's kingdom (Mark 1.10), corresponds to a more intense involvement on earth (v. 12), due in Rev. 12.12 to the shortness of Satan's time (cf. also Dan. 12.1; Acts 2.33). Basic to apocalypticism is the conviction that when the consummation is near, victory will come only after intensified struggle. The inauguration of the kingdom in history is for the purpose of bringing to an end the 'present evil aeon' and introducing the 'coming aeon'. Therefore the kingdom's Spirit embodied in Jesus plunges into the encounter. An essential part of the eschatological hope is the overthrow of the devil.[1] Only in this sense can we understand the action of the Spirit in driving Jesus to the wilderness as depicted here, and the inclusion of the temptation narrative in Mark's introduction at all.

## D. THE CENTRAL MEANING OF THE INTRODUCTION FOR MARK'S GOSPEL

The Marcan introduction seems to have the purpose of presenting the inauguration of eschatological history in the baptism and temptation of Jesus. A more specific definition of Mark's conception of this eschatological history can be gained by investigating those traits which occur both in John's prophecy and in the two-fold fulfilment in baptism and temptation. For it must be in terms of such common factors that the whole presentation in vv. 7–13 finds its organizing principle and its central meaning for Mark. Terminologically it is the 'Spirit' (vv. 8, 10,

[1] Cf. Messel, *Die Einheitlichkeit der jüdischen Eschatologie*, 1915, 171 ff.

12) which gives unity to the three sections.[1] Therefore a clarification of the significance of the 'Spirit' in the introduction will serve to indicate the approach of Mark to the history he has begun to narrate.

The point of departure for an adequate interpretation is the fact that the term Spirit had in the Old Testament and Judaism a strong accent upon the idea of power.[2] This connotation of power is still vivid in Mark's use of the term 'Spirit', as is clearly evident at 1.12; 3.29 f.[3] In both passages the 'Spirit' operates as power: in 1.12 the 'Spirit' 'drives' (ἐκβάλλειν) Jesus into the wilderness; and in 3.29 the 'Spirit' is identified as the power operative in Jesus' 'driving out' demons 3.22 f. (also ἐκβάλλειν).[4] This relation of the πνεῦμα to power serves to give unity to the prophecy of John concerning one who is 'stronger' and who also baptizes 'with the Holy Spirit'. The superior strength is due to the power of the 'Spirit'.

Although Jesus' strength is compared in the prophecy with John's, Mark does not mean that they are competitors one against another, but

---

[1] The accentuation of differences in the conception and rôle of the 'spirit' in these three passages—cf., e.g., Lohmeyer, *Comm.*—can apply only to the pre-Marcan meaning of the allusions. On the background of the general rarity of the term πνεῦμα in Mark and the formal and material proximity of the three occurrences in 1.8–12, this term must be conceived of from Mark's point of view as having the same basic meaning throughout the context, and consequently as providing a line of connexion—not disunity—for the passage.

[2] A clear example is Micah 3.8: 'But as for me, I am filled with power, with the Spirit of the Lord, and with justice and might . . .' A Jewish parallel contemporary with Mark is Josephus, *Ant.* 8.408: γνώσεσθε δ᾽ εἴπερ ἐστὶν ἀληθὴς καὶ τοῦ θείου πνεύματος ἔχει τὴν δύναμιν. The nearness of the two concepts of spirit and power is also confirmed by their association in the following passages: Luke 1.17, where John the Baptist comes ἐν πνεύματι καὶ δυνάμει Ἡλίου; Luke 4.14, where Jesus comes ἐν τῇ δυνάμει τοῦ πνεύματος; Acts 10.38 . . . ἔχρισεν αὐτὸν ὁ θεὸς πνεύματι ἁγίῳ καὶ δυνάμει; I Cor. 2.4 . . . ἐν ἀποδείξει πνεύματος καὶ δυνάμεως; Rom. 15.19 δύναμις πνεύματος; II Tim. 1.7, . . . πνεῦμα τῆς δυνάμεως Cf. the presentation by Grundmann, *Der Begriff der Kraft in der neutestamentlichen Gedankenwelt,* 1932, esp. 56.

[3] Cf. E. Schweizer, 'The Spirit of Power', *Interpretation,* VI (1952), 260, and in his forthcoming article on πνεῦμα in the *TWNT,* VI. He points (261 f.) to the fact that the prophecy of John is not understood by Mark as the apocalyptic judgement of wind (πνεῦμα) and fire (cf. Matt. and Luke), but rather is brought into conformity to the early Christian idea of the πνεῦμα as the power of God within the eschatological history, evident in Jesus and promised (Mark 13.11) to the Church.

[4] This is the normal Marcan term for exorcisms: performed by Jesus: 1.34; 7.26; by disciples: 3.15; 6.13; 9.18, 28, 38.

rather that Jesus' strength exceeds John's against the common foe. The greater strength prophesied by John and fulfilled at Jesus' baptism with the Spirit is demonstrated at the temptation. This relation of the designation 'strong' to the struggle with Satan finds its confirmation and nearest parallel in the exorcism debate, the only other place in Mark where the term 'strong' recurs. Satan is called (3.27) the 'strong one' against whom Jesus struggles, in language based on the prophecy of Isa. 49.24 ff.[1] Jesus is not here named 'stronger', but the fact that he binds and plunders the 'strong one' makes the fact of his superior strength evident. Therefore the same passage concerning exorcism where the power of the Spirit is evident (see above), also indicates that this power is used against the strong Satan. Thus is revealed the inherent connexion between these two passages, and between the ideas of 'strength' and 'Spirit'.

The fact that the terms 'stronger', 'Spirit', and 'Satan' at the centre of the prologue form a coherent meaning of eschatological struggle has been confirmed by the exorcism debate, where all three elements recur. Clearly the explanation of the exorcisms in 3.21–30 is a close parallel in its theological meaning to the Marcan introduction. The struggle which took place in the temptation continues in the exorcisms of the Marcan narrative,[2] and the single event of the temptation becomes in the exorcisms an extended history of redemptive significance. This fact is of some relevance for the discussion in a subsequent chapter of history after A.D. 30 in Mark. For once the saving action of Jesus over Satan is divided into a series of stories, it has lost its single-event character and is already on the way to becoming a history open to potential continuation within the Church.

In view of the close relation between the baptism-temptation unit and the exorcism debate, the question arises as to why the baptism and temptation are separated from the body of the narrative by the new beginning at 1.14–15. This trait lets the reader sense not only a continuity, but a discontinuity, and indicates that the introduction is not

---

[1]Cf. Otto, *The Kingdom of God and the Son of Man*, 100 ff.

[2]Lightfoot, *History and Interpretation in the Gospels*, 65, erroneously sees in the temptation the whole of the preliminary struggle with evil which apocalypticism expected just before the end. His error is due to the fact that he interprets 1.15 as 'realized eschatology', i.e., the kingdom has (already) 'come upon you', so that the struggle preceding the kingdom must be terminated prior to 1.15.

merely the first in a series, but also the foundation of the series. Although the succeeding episodes flow uninterruptedly from one to the other, they are together separated from the introduction. John had disappeared from the narrative much earlier, so that the desire to separate John from Jesus could have been met without reintroducing him for this purpose (1.14; cf. Luke) nor is this John-motif central in the new introduction. Therefore the question must be raised as to whether there is not some further facet in the early Christian understanding of Jesus' history which Mark expresses by this line of separation.

It has already been suggested that the announcement in 1.15: 'the time *has* been fulfilled and the kingdom of God *has* drawn near', provides a first commentary on the baptism-temptation unit. Since this announcement is presented thematically at the opening of the public ministry, it tends to define the baptism-temptation unit as the basis presupposed by—and in this sense set off from—the whole public ministry of Jesus. It has become clear that the baptism-temptation unit finds its closest parallel in the exorcism debate. Therefore it would seem consistent to see in 3.27 a further allusion, even more specific than that in 1.14 f., to the relation between the introduction and the public ministry: 'no one can enter the house of the strong one and plunder his goods, unless he first binds the strong one [introduction, esp. the temptation], and then he can plunder his house [narrative, esp. the exorcisms].'[1]

Such a two-fold time reference with regard to the eschatological attack upon evil spirits is documented in the Testament of Levi 18.12: 'And Beliar shall be bound [Mark: "first bind the strong one"] by him and he will give power to his children to tread upon the evil spirits.' The fact that such a two-fold construction of Jesus' activity prior to his

---

[1]This exegesis has been challenged by Klostermann (*Comm.*, 2nd. ed.), who identifies the σκευή with the exorcised demons rather than the freed humans, and thus identifies the act of binding with the act of exorcism. However, Grundmann (*Der Begriff der Kraft in der neutestamentlichen Gedankenwelt*, 49 f.) has shown on the basis of Isa. 49.25; Test. Levi 18.12; Test. Zeb. 9.8; Jub. 10.8; Luke 13.16, that the 'booty' is more likely to be the humans involved. Klostermann then (3rd and 4th ed.) conceded the point in principle, but continued to maintain his interpretation of Mark 3.27 as an exception. His remaining arguments have already been answered in the discussion above. The assumption of H.-D. Wendland, *Die Eschatologie des Reiches Gottes bei Jesus*, 1931, 49, that the 'binding' refers to exorcism and the 'plundering' to the *parousia*, is negated by the fact—which Wendland himself conceded—that the exorcisms are not causal presuppositions of the *parousia*.

passion was envisaged in the early Church is demonstrated by Acts 10.38, which could very well be a commentary on Mark 3.27: 'how God anointed Jesus of Nazareth with the Holy Spirit and with power; how he went about doing good and healing all that were oppressed by the devil, for God was with him'. In so far as Mark's presentation of Jesus' life conforms to Acts 10.38, his understanding of Jesus' history can be accurately called '*kerygmatic*' in the stricter sense of dependence upon the early sermon's outline.[1]

It is probable that both kinds of time reference in this motif of the *kerygma* are rooted in teachings of the historical Jesus. Present references have been identified as authentic by most scholars for some time; past references are less obvious, but may also be detected.[2] It is this old tradition of an inaugural action prior to the public ministry, making it possible and serving as its basis and theme, which finds expression in the Marcan introduction. This tradition points to the coming of the Spirit and an initial victory over Satan, which are also the constituent elements in the theological meaning of the Marcan introduction. In this initial encounter between the eschatological Spirit and the ruler of the present evil aeon, the kingdom of God draws near. This event marks the 'beginning' of the last hour and thus of the Christian history (1.1). The basis has been provided for the ministry of Jesus, which consists in proclaiming the new situation (1.15), and in carrying through the struggle against Satan in the power of the Spirit.

[1]C. H. Dodd, 'The Framework of the Gospel Narrative', *ET*, XLIII (1931–2), 396–400, and *The Apostolic Preaching*, 1936, 46–51 of 2nd ed. (1944), has drawn attention to the public ministry in the *kerygma* as the outline upon which Mark was written. But he has not done justice to the fact that the *kerygma* does not outline any succession or order of events in the Galilean ministry to support the supposedly *kerygmatic* outline he finds in the Marcan summaries. The reference in Acts 10.38 to 'doing good' and exorcizing is hardly intended as a chronological order, and if it were, it would not correspond to the Marcan presentation. However the *kerygma* does distinguish the public ministry as a whole from the baptism with which it begins and the passion with which it ends.

[2]Cf. my article on 'Jesus' Understanding of History', *JBR*, XXIII (1955), 17–24, where such a past reference is traced in the eschatological parables of Jesus. Cf. also Luke 10.18; Matt. 11.11a, 12; 21.32; Mark 11.30, as well as the echoes of John's teachings in Jesus' sayings.

# V

# THE EXORCISM NARRATIVES

## A. THE DIRECTION OF THE INVESTIGATION

The term 'cosmic language' refers to specific allusions by Mark to the cosmic forces which transcend historical immanence and yet participate in the history Mark records. The introduction to Mark has made it clear that Mark speaks in cosmic language of a struggle between the Spirit and Satan. In distinction to the mass scenes and human milieu which characterize the ministry of John the Baptist, Jesus was presented as solitary, addressed privately from heaven as if John the Baptist were no longer present, and then driven into the solitude of the wilderness for the temptation. Jesus' context is the cosmic language of the opened heavens, the voice of God, the Son of God, the Spirit, Satan, angels and beasts. When this aspect of the introduction is envisaged, the expectation could arise that the Marcan narrative to follow would be more myth than history. The movement from the Baptist's crowds to the wilderness could seem introductory to 'war in heaven', 'Michael and his angels fighting against the dragon' (Rev. 12.7 ff.). The exorcisms which have already been related to the introduction would then serve as the nearest rapprochement of a mythological narrative to historical events. The 'eschatological history' would hardly be history at all. Only when this alternative is clearly envisaged can one evaluate properly the actual state of the facts with regard to the cosmic language in Mark and the actual rôle of the exorcisms in the narrative. Cosmic language is rare in Mark, occurring primarily at decisive points of the narratives; the exorcisms, rather than being the nearest point of approach to history in a myth, are the points in a historical narrative where the transcendent meaning of that history is most clearly evident.

Mark's references in the exorcism debate (3.22 ff.) to the action of the Spirit through Jesus or the action of Satan through the demoniac are only partially 'cosmic' in language. Therefore the key in which the narration is set is somewhat more subdued. The exorcism stories themselves refer to 'demons' and 'evil spirits', and to Jesus as 'Son of God'. They are put into the context of the struggle between the Spirit and Satan by the debate in 3.22 ff. Yet the exorcism stories nowhere allude to the Spirit and Satan, nor are the other cosmic terms of the introduction to the Gospel encountered. Rather the exorcisms are in several respects more historical in form of presentation. In distinction from Satan at the temptation, the demons who encounter Jesus are never disembodied, but are rather in possession of humans through whose organs they speak. The historical cast of the exorcism stories is also evident from the fact that the scenes are presented as public, not esoteric, taking place in the synagogue (1.23, 39), or in a tumultuous crowd (3.7–12; 1.32–34; 9.14–27), or in such a way as to draw public attention (5.14–20; [9, 38]). Exorcism was often accompanied by preaching (1.39; 3.14 f.; [5.19 f.]; 6.13), or teaching (1.21–28), or healing (1.32–34; 6.13; 3.10–11). When Mark carries the cosmic struggle from the solitary encounter with Satan at the temptation into the historical setting of the exorcism narratives, it is already evident that he proposes to describe the cosmic struggle as taking place in historical occurrence.

The struggles between the demoniacs and the Son of God are sufficiently historical in tone to serve as a bridge between the passages with predominantly cosmic language and the narratives where the language remains more completely within immanent categories of human debate and conflict. The central position of the struggle with demoniacs serves to show on the one hand that the cosmic-language passages have very much to do with history and are really a form employed by Mark for stating a theological understanding of history. On the other hand these historical struggles with demoniacs provide a working hypothesis for interpreting the debates with opponents: although cast in more immanent language, these debates are not intended as only immanent or relativistic by Mark, but represent for him the same eschatological struggle in history. The sharpness of the debates as a matter of life and death for Jesus is simply a subdued form of expression for the cosmic struggle taking place in them. This most historical form of expression thus maintains the same sense of unreserved involvement expressed by the cosmic language.

We have identified three levels of Marcan language, which could be summarized schematically as follows: the Spirit and Satan; the Son of God and demoniacs; Jesus and his opponents. The three-fold classification of Marcan language cannot be pressed, but does provide an avenue of approach into the Marcan material by means of which Mark's central understanding of history can be traced into the more immanently-phrased parts of the narrative.[1]

### B. THE EXORCISMS AS A DUALISTIC COSMIC STRUGGLE

The exorcisms are interpreted in 3.22–30 in terms of the cosmic struggle between the Spirit and Satan begun in the temptation. The exorcism narratives themselves do not refer specifically to the Spirit and Satan. But they reveal the presence of the same struggle by the sharply hostile and antithetic form in which the stories are presented. For at one important point the exorcism narratives differ from modern historical style: they do not presuppose the ultimate ambiguity or relativity of historical occurrence.

The personages in the exorcism narratives are designated in such a way to make clear their opposing rôles in the cosmic struggle. Mark describes the demoniac as a 'man with an unclean spirit' (1.23; 5.2), or a person who 'has' an 'unclean spirit' (7.25) or a 'dumb spirit' (9.17). For Mark, the diagnosis consists simply in the presence of the demon, and he gives the fact of the demon a prominent place throughout his presentation.[2] The identifications of Jesus as 'Son ['holy one' 1.24] of God' (3.11; 5.7) also render the contrasting nature of the two antagonists evident. It is possible that the unusual term 'holy one of God' (1.24) is an allusion to Jesus as bearer of the 'Holy Spirit' (1.8) over

---

[1] A somewhat parallel procedure is followed by Wilhelm Wrede, *Das Messiasgeheimnis in den Evangelien*, 2, 7, when he bases his argument for a theological approach pervading Mark upon the accentuation of those passages which he regarded as the most 'unhistorical': the baptism, the resurrection of Jairus' daughter, the two miraculous feedings, Jesus walking on the water, the transfiguration, the angels with the women at the tomb. His argument is to the effect that a narrative including such incidents must be pervaded throughout by an attitude different from that of the objective historian, i.e., by a theological attitude. However the present study differs from Wrede in that it does not ignore as irrelevant the historically-cast bulk of the narrative.

[2] Demon: 1.34, 39; 3.15, 22; 6.13; 7.26, 29, 30; 9.38; unclean spirit, in addition to the above: 1.26, 27; 3.11, 30; 5.8, 13; 6.7; 9.25; spirit: 9.20; dumb and deaf spirit: 9.25.

against the 'unclean spirit' (1.23, 26 f.).[1] Such a contrast between the two kinds of spirit is explicit in 3.29 f.

Jesus' refutation (3.22–30) of the scribal charge that he is possessed by Beelzebub serves to stop any confusion as to the nature of Jesus' super-human power, and concentrates the attention upon the contrast between the antagonists. All the demonic forces are united under Satan (vv. 23, 26). Any friendship to Jesus on their part is excluded by the reference to the fall of a divided kingdom (v. 24) or house (v. 25). Any friendship to the demons on the part of Jesus is excluded by the saying that a plunderer must first have bound the owner of the house (v. 27). Jesus' action is attributed to the Holy Spirit (v. 29). The rarity of this identification in Mark shows the importance the present issue has for him. This importance is also stressed by the designation of the scribal confusion as an unpardonable or eternal sin (v. 29).

The clear-cut antithesis between the personages in the exorcism narratives is accentuated by the hostile attitude in which their discussions take place. We do not find calm conversations, but shouts and orders. The demons 'shout' at Jesus: 1.23; 3.11; (5.5); 5.7; 9.26. In 5.7 the demon 'adjures' Jesus. Jesus 'orders' the demons (1.27; 9.25), or 'reproaches' them with an order (1.25; 3.12; 9.25). The only passage approaching normal conversation is in 5.9–13, after the struggle is over and the authoritative word of exorcism had been uttered (v. 8). This conversation does not serve to place Jesus and the demons in 'normal' relations, but rather to accentuate the completeness of Jesus' victory, a trait which recurs normally in the Marcan narratives. Jesus is not communing with the demon, he is disposing of him. The communion takes place with the liberated human (vv. 15 ff.).

The hostility which Mark expresses in his descriptions of the conversations is confirmed by an examination of what was said. Bauernfeind has shown[2] that the three sayings spoken by demons to Jesus (1.24; 3.11; 5.7) are all closely parallel to incantations of witchcraft in the magical papyri and elsewhere.[3] Therefore the words could very well

---

[1]Cf. Procksch, *TWNT*, I, 102. This interpretation is more probable than Lagrange's reference, *Évangile selon St. Marc*, 2nd ed., 1928, to the character of Jesus, or Taylor's reference to a content of Jesus' preaching which the demon had supposedly heard.

[2]*Die Worte der Dämonen in Markusevangelium*, 3 ff.

[3]Bauernfeind lists parallels to the οἶδά σε form (14 f.) and of the σὺ εἶ form (21 ff.) of address. The purpose is to get magical control of the person so addressed.

for Mark and his readers give the impression of a defensive magical incantation. This hostility is of course only accentuated by the reference in the demon's sayings to Jesus 'destroying' (1.24) or 'tormenting' (5.7) them, as well as by the opening challenge (1.24; 5.7): 'What have you to do with us?' In 5.7 the demon appeals to God against Jesus, in language commonly used *against* demons: ὁρκίζω σε τὸν θεόν.[1]

We should not be deterred from this hostile interpretation by the 'confession' that Jesus is the 'Holy One of God' (1.24), 'Son of God' (3.11), 'Son of the Most High God' (5.7). One may compare the 'confession' (12.13 f.) of the Pharisees and Herodians to Jesus as the ideal teacher, where their intention is specifically stated to be that of 'ensnaring' him. It is worthy of note that the 'confessions' of the demons are not limited to Jesus' title, but also reveal his rôle, 1.24: 'thou hast come to destroy us'. The statement does not refer simply to the coming of Jesus from Nazareth to the synagogue of Capernaum, but describes Jesus' coming to earth as a heavenly mission to destroy the demons, and thus reflects the cosmic scope of the struggle.[2] Here the loftiness of Jesus' person is seen not as an end in itself, but in its significance for the historical struggle in which he is involved. Similarly the other lofty designation of Jesus as 'Son of God' is not to be understood simply as an innocuous honorific title, but as a term with ominous implications for the demons. The term had been closely associated with Satan's opponent the Spirit in 1.10–12. Therefore the content of the demons' confessions reveals the impossibility of understanding these 'confessions' as friendly or reverent. Their purpose is rather to gain power over Jesus by using his secret, spirit-world name.

The fact that the demons kneel (5.6) and fall down (3.11) before Jesus does not eliminate the hostility of their intentions or render their 'confessions' devout. These gestures are recognition of the superior power of Jesus, and as such are servile. But they do not end the hostility of the demons, as the analysis of their words has shown. Rather the gesture provides the demons with the occasion for attempting to overcome Jesus' power by naming his name, or even by adjuring by God. Only when these attacks fail do they plead for the mercy which

[1]Deissmann, *Bible Studies*, 274 ff.
[2]Cf. similarly 1.38; 2.17; 10.45 for the identification of various facets of Jesus' ministry as the purpose of his 'coming'.

their posture suggests (5.10–12), or perform a last act of defiance which reveals their real attitude (1.26).

The fact that Jesus silences[1] the demons' 'confessions' (1.25, 34; 3.11), and proceeds to cast them out (1.25; 5.8), confirms the inacceptability of their attitude. The act of exorcism is the characteristic attitude toward the demons mentioned with regard to Jesus: 1.34, 39; 3.22 f.; (7.26); (9.38); and his disciples: 3.15; 6.13; (9.18, 28, 38). Exorcism is specifically designated as 'plundering' in 3.27. The only reference in Mark to demon or unclean spirit which is not accompanied by an explicit exorcism is 3.11 f., where in a summary passage Jesus' command to be silent suffices. A further indication of Jesus' opposition is to be discerned in 9.38–40, where the disciples do not want to recognize as an ally a person casting out demons in Jesus' name, since the person is not an official disciple. Jesus, recognizing the existence of only two sides, reverses their decision and declares that such action proves the person in question to be on Jesus' side: 'No one who does wonders in my name is able soon to speak ill of me. For he who is not against us is for us.' Thus Jesus' attitude confirms the original accusation of the demons (1.24): 'You have come to destroy us.' Prior to the Marcan context, and apart from the commentary in 3.22 ff., the exorcism stories resembled many exorcism stories of the ancient world, and could have been understood in the same non-eschatological way (cf. Matt. 12.27 par.). In the Marcan presentation they depict a cosmic struggle in history to inaugurate the eschatological reign of God.

---

[1]Even Wrede, *Messiasgeheimnis*, 33, n. 1, concedes with regard to 1.25: 'Φιμώθητι does not in and of itself say that Jesus does not desire the messianic address; rather he simply strikes down the demon's self-assertion evident in his speech. In 4.39 Jesus says the same thing to the sea.' But then Wrede adds: 'Nevertheless the evangelist seems, in view of the parallels [!], to mean that Jesus by his reply also rejects the messianic address.' Cf. Bauernfeind, *Die Worte der Dämonen im Markusevangelium*, 31; Ebeling, *Messiasgeheimnis*, 128 ff.: 'Against the demonstrated intention of the demon . . .' Wrede (37), maintains that the reason for silencing demons cannot be their demonic nature, since this explanation would not apply to the silencings following the raising of Jairus' daughter (5.43) and the healing of the deaf-mute (7.36). But Wrede forces this parallel at the expense of ignoring the contrast between the hostility in the commands to demons and the absence of such hostility in the other cases. Furthermore the basic assumption of Wrede (36), that all the silencings in Mark must be understood in the same way, is open to serious question, in view of the variety in form and mood of the silencings.

## C. THE OUTCOME OF THE EXORCISM STRUGGLES

The exorcism narratives have been seen to present a contrast between the personages of these scenes, which helped to identify in them the continuation of the cosmic struggle within history. However there is a second contrast within the exorcism stories: that between the violence and destructiveness of the demon in the human he possesses, and the tranquillity and communion in the scenes of Jesus with the liberated person. An analysis of this contrast will make it evident that Mark's understanding of history not only includes the presence of the cosmic struggle, but also the presence at places within history of the victory and of the resultant idyllic status which follows upon that struggle and victory.

The actions of the demons are violent, directed toward injury and death. In 5.3-5 the demon's violence is such as to break all chains and foot bonds, and he cannot be tamed. The demoniac lives among tombs and mountains, crying out and bruising himself with stones. In 9.17, 25 the demon has rendered the boy deaf and dumb; it casts him down, causing him to foam, grind his teeth and become rigid (v. 18); it casts him into the fire and into water to destroy him (v. 22). The swine rush into the sea and are drowned (5.13), after the legion of demons enters them. This violence is only accentuated by the presence of Jesus. His command of exorcism produces convulsions and shouting (1.26; 9.26). At the sight of Jesus the demon convulses the epileptic boy, who, falling on the ground, rolls about foaming (9.20). After the exorcism the boy became like a corpse and the crowd took him for dead (9.26).

The close association of this violence to physical harm and death is relevant to Mark's understanding of the crucifixion and resurrection. The sudden reversal of the situation as the passion narrative is replaced by the Easter story is already anticipated in the exorcism stories, and here the shift is identified as due to the victory over the demon, i.e., Satan. Following upon the act of exorcism, the scene is depicted so as to make it evident that violence and death itself have been cast out. Jesus' cure of the epileptic boy is described in terms of resurrection: ὁ δὲ Ἰησοῦς κρατήσας τῆς χειρὸς αὐτοῦ ἤγειρεν αὐτόν, καὶ ἀνέστη, 9.27 (cf. also 5.41 f.). The contrast between the two states is also sharply drawn at the end of the story of the Gerasene demoniac, where (5.15) the liberated man is seen with Jesus 'seated, clothed, and in his right mind', and the remark is specifically made that this is 'he who had had Legion'. Jesus sends him back to his family to proclaim his liberation (5.19) whereas the demon had forced him to make his home among the tombs (vv. 2 f., 5).

In addition to the exorcisms, other miracle stories accentuate the contrast between the situation before and after the cure. It is appropriate to envisage these miracle stories of Mark as a continuation of the same struggle as that carried on in the exorcisms. Judaism normally attributed various kinds of disease and misfortune to the action of demons.[1] Furthermore there are traces of exorcism language in three of the other Marcan miracle stories: 1.43 καὶ ἐμβριμησάμενος αὐτῷ εὐθὺς ἐξέβαλεν αὐτόν; 4.39 ἐπετίμησεν τῷ ἀνέμῳ καὶ εἶπεν τῇ θαλάσσῃ σιώπα, πεφίμωσο; 7.35: καὶ εὐθὺς ἐλύθη ὁ δεσμὸς τῆς γλώσσης αὐτοῦ. The similarity in language to the exorcisms is evident from the fact that ἐκβάλλειν (1.43)[2] occurs of exorcisms in 1.34, 39; 3.15, 22 f.; 6.13; 7.26; 9.18, 28; ἐπιτιμᾶν (4.39) occurs addressed to demons in 1.25; 3.12; 9.25;[3] φιμοῦν (4.39) occurs as the command to demons in 1.25; and δεῖν (7.35) occurs in 3.27 to describe Jesus' action making exorcism possible.[4]

In spite of the nearness of miracle stories to exorcisms, the hostile opposition which characterized the exorcism narratives is largely lacking from those miracle stories which are not specifically exorcisms.

[1]Cf. Foerster, *TWNT*, II, 13 f.

[2]Lohmeyer remarks that ἐκβάλλειν alone is not a technical expression for exorcism, and that the object αὐτόν refers to the leper, not a demon. This indicates that an exorcism is not intended in the Marcan text as it now stands. However in view of the varied conjectures as to textual corruptions and conflation of stories (Lohmeyer himself conjectures the latter!), attention needs to be called to the fact that the story of the leper contains a verse largely unintelligible in its present setting, but admirably suited to an exorcism narrative. Even on the basis of the text as it now stands, the anger of Jesus can only be explained in terms of his opposition to the combined forces of disease, death, sin, and Satan. Cf. Campbell Bonner, 'Traces of Thaumaturgic Technique in the Miracles', *Harvard Theological Review*, XX (1927), 171–81, and Kirsopp Lake, ΈΜΒΡΙΜΗΣΑΜΕΝΟΣ and 'ΟΡΓΙΣΘΕΙΣ, Mark 1.40–43', *HTR*, XVI (1923), 197–8.

[3]Cf. Stauffer, *TWNT*, II, 623.

[4]Further parallels from outside Mark tend to confirm this demonic association of the concept of 'binding' and 'loosing': e.g., Luke 13.16; Acts 20.22 Rev. 20.2. Cf. Büchsel, *TWNT*, II, 59 f.; Bauer, *Worterbuch* on δεσμός, δέω; Str-B, I, 739. Further examples, esp. of binding the tongue, are given by Adolf Deissmann, *Light from the Ancient East*, 304–7.

Nevertheless Jesus' opposition to the disease is as much a matter of course as his opposition to the demons. It may be of some significance that the only specific references to hostility in the miracles seem to be in the healing of the leper and the stilling of the storm, two of the instances where the language approaches nearest to that of the exorcisms.

Although hostility is not prominent in the miracle stories, these stories share the other significant trait of exorcism narratives: a sharp contrast between the state before and after the action of Jesus. The compassion-arousing situation of 'the sheep not having a shepherd' combined with the lateness of the hour, the loneliness of the place, the limitation of funds, and the scarcity of food at hand (6.34–38), stands in sharp contrast to 'all' who 'eat and are filled' with much left over, in spite of the vast size of the crowd (6.42–44). In the second feeding there occurs the same emphasis upon a compassion-arousing crowd, which is three days without food and too feeble to reach distant homes without nourishment (8.1–3). One observes also the same deserted location of the scene and the same scarcity of food on hand (vv. 4 f.). This situation is also contrasted with the 'eating and being full', with much left over, in spite of the vast size of the crowd (vv. 8 f.). The amplitude of the food which remains is accentuated as the point of both stories by the discussion in 8.19–21.

In the 'great storm of wind', the waves beat into the boat, which fills with water, so that there is danger of perishing (4.37 f.). This stands in contrast with the winds ceasing and the 'great calm' of v. 39.

When the terminations of miracle stories are not monopolized by other such favourite motifs as the crowd's awe or the unrestrained testimony of the cured person, there is often a motif to accentuate the completeness of the cure: Peter's wife's mother resumes her rôle as hostess (1.31); the leper receives official priestly confirmation of his cure (1.44); the paralytic takes up his bed and walks (2.11 f.); the man with the withered hand stretches it out 'and it was restored' (3.5); the woman with the issue of blood goes 'in peace' and is 'healed of her disease' (5.34); Jairus' daughter eats food (5.43); the deaf mute has his hearing restored, the bond of his tongue is loosened, and he speaks 'correctly' (7.35); the blind man at first sees men as walking trees (8.24), but when Jesus completes the cure he sees everything 'clearly' (v. 25).

Such motifs are inevitable in miracle stories, and have many parallels in other literatures.[1] Yet in some of the scenes the accent upon the fact of a residuum following the action is so accentuated, as in the two feedings, as to surpass what is necessary to prove the fact of the miracle. Furthermore the fact that the cure has the spiritual significance of a restored communion is often accentuated, as in the motif of sending the cured person home (2.11; 5.19; 8.26), as well as the scene with the cured Gerasene demoniac. The outcomes of the cures do not consist in a dedication to the contemplative life outside the course of history, but rather in a restoration to society, a return from seclusion back into the historical process.

The analysis of the exorcisms and other miracle stories brings us to the point from which the remainder of Mark, where demons are not mentioned and the language seems correspondingly more historical, can be understood. Jesus' unrelenting opposition in the exorcism narrative ceases abruptly when the human and the demon are separated. The purpose of this antagonism becomes clear: Jesus is struggling for life and communion on behalf of the possessed person. Both of these characteristics of a true historical existence had been opposed by the demon. These scenes which are nearest to the cosmic scene of the baptism and temptation have not by this fact turned us away from history. Rather, they have served to present the understanding of history not only underlying the exorcisms, but, as we are subsequently to investigate, also the whole of Mark's narrative. For Mark, history is not ultimately ambiguous or relativistic; rather it has two clear-cut and irreconcilable alternatives in it, which can at times be stated as simply as Son of God *versus* demon, Holy Spirit *versus* unclean spirit. Because of this clear alternative in history, struggle between the two opposing objectives of life or death, communion or segregation, is understandable. Only if history offered no real alternatives and no real results would inaction, 'other-worldliness' and resignation be appropriate. It is Jesus' function to enter this struggle on behalf of the true destiny of mankind and with his heavenly power to carry through to the victory, and to the life and communion it brings.

[1]Cf. esp. Dibelius, *From Tradition to Gospel*, chap. IV, 'Tales', 70–103.

# VI

# FROM THE DEBATES TO THE RESURRECTION

## A. THE RELATION OF THE DEBATES TO THE EXORCISMS

It has become clear that the exorcisms are understood by Mark in terms of the cosmic struggle inaugurated at the baptism and temptation of Jesus. Thus a bridgehead has been established within the body of the Marcan narrative for the thesis that this historical narrative is itself envisaged in terms of that cosmic struggle. The validity of this thesis depends upon whether or not the remainder of the Marcan narrative material, when cosmic language and references to demons are lacking, is intended as a continuation of that cosmic struggle. It is in terms of this question that the discussion now turns to the debates within Mark. For they not only form an important segment of Marcan material, but are also closely related to the exorcisms on the one hand and to the remainder of the Marcan narrative on the other.

The debates have been subjected to formal analysis by the form critics. Most of them were treated among the 'paradigms' by Dibelius,[1] but a separate category of '*Streitgespräche*' (lit. 'conflict discussions', or 'disputes'), was identified by Albertz[2] and Bultmann.[3] The latter term is a more accurate designation of their original '*Sitz im Leben*', inasmuch as rabbinic parallels[4] make it evident that the form arose within the setting of public debate, not in the cultic atmosphere of the sermon for believers. The debates do lead to a significant saying of Jesus of illustrative ('paradigmatic') value; yet it is of equal relevance that this saying is the climax of a struggle. The truth of God is not given as didactic exposition, but as the result of conflict, attained through effort, and as evidence of a break-through in the attack against evil.[5] This is the case both in the debates with Jesus' opponents and in the

[1] *From Tradition to Gospel*, 37 ff.
[2] *Die synoptischen Streitgespräche*, 1921.
[3] *Die Geschichte der synoptischen Tradition*, 2. Aufl., 39 ff.
[4] Cf. Bultmann, 42 ff.
[5] Cf. Ebeling, *Messiasgeheimnis*, 55.

debates with his disciples. In this sense Bultmann's association of the *Streit- und Schulgespräche* is preferable to Albertz' exclusion of the debates with disciples. On the other hand Dibelius is right[1] in pointing out that some of the Marcan debates (3.22–30; 7.5–23; 10.2–12) do not present the same form as those designated '*Streitgespräche*', so that as a matter of fact there is no single form for the debates in Mark. The present discussion on the Marcan debates is not limited to those conforming to any one 'form', but embraces all the Marcan debates.

The *Streitgespräche* in their pre-Marcan oral form are similar to the rabbinic debates.[2] However Mark is not concerned to maintain this set form. This is particularly evident in the case of the debate about ceremonial cleanliness (7.1 ff.). Furthermore Mark envisages a basic distinction between Jesus' teaching and that of the rabbis (1.22: 'not as the scribes'). For Mark, the nearest parallel to Jesus' debates is not the rabbinic debate, but rather the exorcism. This is evident from the fact that he chooses an exorcism story in the synagogue (1.23 ff.) to illustrate Jesus' unusual synagogal teaching which has 'authority' (1.22). This encounter with the demon includes violent debate, so that its summary (1.27) not only repeats the 'authority' motif, but also repeats the concept of a 'new teaching'. Thus Mark provides the exorcism as the pattern for interpreting the debates in the synagogues.[3]

There is also a similarity of form between the exorcisms and the debates. The demon advances upon Jesus with a hostile challenge, only to be silenced by an authoritative word of Jesus (1.23–26; 3.11 f.). The debates with the Jewish authorities likewise begin normally with a hostile question or accusation of the opponent, which is frustrated by Jesus' definitive reply: 2.6–11; 2.16–17; 2.18–22; 2.24–28; 3.2–5; 7.5–15; 8.11–12; 12.18–27. Sometimes his reply consists in taking the initiative, which calls forth a further statement of the opposition before Jesus' final word: 10.2–9; 11.27–33; 12.13–17. The same phenomenon occurs in the exorcism of 5.6–13.[4] Jesus' initiative is also accentuated by those

[1]*From Tradition to Gospel*, 222.
[2]Cf. Bultmann, *Die Geschichte der synoptischen Tradition*, 2. Aufl., 42 ff.
[3]Dibelius, *From Tradition to Gospel*, 43, classifies 1.23 ff. among the 'less pure' paradigms, and thus associates this exorcism with the debates. Albertz, *Die synoptischen Streitgespräche*, 152, recognized the association of the debates with the exorcisms.
[4]Cf. Albertz' summary of the form of the *Streitgespräche*, *Die Botschaft des Neuen Testaments*, I, 1 (1947), 67 f., which could equally well characterize the exorcisms.

scenes where the accusing question was addressed to the disciples but not to him (2.16), or where it was not spoken aloud at all (2.6 f.; 3.2), but is nevertheless drawn out and refuted by Jesus. A similar shift from the disciples to Jesus is present in the exorcism story of 9.14 ff. The discussions with disciples or 'neutrals' do not display such overt hostility as do the exorcisms; yet the rejection of a false understanding and the affirmation of a clearcut and definitively true understanding is maintained: 3.31–35; 6.2–4; 7.14–15, 17–23; 8.27–30, 31–33; 9.38–40; 10.13–16, 17–22, 35–45; 13.1–2; 14.3–9. Thus there is considerable formal similarity between the exorcisms and the debates. It would be an error to associate the exorcisms only with the miracles, as if the healing action were the only constitutive element in the exorcism. This would be an all too medical interpretation of the exorcisms, and to this extent a modernization. The exorcisms are also struggles of minds, or will, and consist in words, as well as action. They culminate in an authoritative saying, with which the issue is settled. All these are points of similarity to the debates.

It is true that the exorcisms are drawn into close association with the healings by the fact that diseases (and other natural evils such as storms) were associated with the action of demons, so that there is not too great a distinction between an exorcism and other miracles in Mark. But an examination of the debates in Mark makes it clear that there is also an intimate relationship of meaning between the exorcisms and the debates. Just as there are traces of exorcism language in the miracle stories,[1] there are equally clear indications in the debates that they too are the action of Satan. The debates with the Jewish authorities are designated 'temptations' (8.11; 10.2; 12.15), thus making their diabolic instigation clear. The debates with the disciples concerning the passion are put into this context by the pointed attribution of the disciples' attitude to Satan (8.33), and the designation of the danger to which they are exposed in view of the passion as 'temptation' (14.38).

The cosmic struggle has here reached a more subtle form and is stated in more immanent language than was the case in the exorcisms.

---

[1] The 'sigh' which in the miracle story (7.34) is an 'expression of collected strength' having parallels in the magical papyri (Bauer, *Wörterbuch*, 4. Aufl., on στενάζω), recurs in a debate with the Jewish authorities (8.12). Cf. C. Bonner, 'Traces of Thaumaturgic Technique in the Miracles', *HTR*, XX (1927), 171–81.

But just as was the case there, Mark is not concerned either with purely immanent temptations, nor with purely inward and mental temptations; rather the concept is that of 'trials' instigated by Satan and consisting in a historical encounter in a specific situation.[1] It is therefore evident that Mark not only presents the debates in a form similar to that of the exorcisms, but also envisages the meaning of the debates in a way similar to the exorcisms. The debates are a continuation of the cosmic struggle initiated at the baptism and temptation and carried into the narrative of Jesus' public ministry first by the exorcisms.

B. THE TRUTH OF ESCHATOLOGICAL HISTORY IN THE DEBATES

The tendency of the debates with Jewish authorities is to attack the ambiguity of a historical situation whose truth is confused by the evil intentions of the opposition. Jesus reduces the confusion to clarity so as to reveal the truth inherent in the historical situation. Just as in the debate concerning exorcism, the affirmation of the truth of history is rooted in the affirmation of the presence of eschatology in history.

Both the break-through to the truth of history and its eschatological basis are apparent in the first group of Marcan debates (2.1–3.6). When Jesus forgives sin, he is charged with 'blasphemy', for 'who is able to forgive sins except one, God?' (2.7). This confused interpretation is answered categorically (2.10): 'The Son of Man has authority to forgive sins on earth.' Here clarity is reached not in terms of a general principle, but rather in terms of the presence of the eschatological Son of Man in history. The confusing implication that 'eating with tax gatherers and sinners' means advocating sin, is clarified as the action of the 'doctor', who is 'calling' sinners (2.16 f.). The illustration of the doctor is not left as a general principle, but rather is focused on the 'coming' of Jesus. The accusation of impiety in not fasting is clarified by stating that the mournful significance of fasting is inappropriate during (eschatological) marriage celebrations (2.19). The antithesis is further clarified by the distinction between a 'patch of unshrunk cloth'

---

[1]Compare the Rabbinic understanding of Satan's tempting activity, Messel, *Die Einheitlichkeit der jüdischen Eschatologie*, 179. Illustrations are given by Weber, *System der altsynagogalen palästinischen Theologie*, 1880, 243. The gentile environment with its temptation to hellenize is an example of Satan's activity (Messel, 163 ff.).

and an 'old coat' (v. 21), and the distinction of 'new wine' from 'old skins' (v. 22). Thus the true conduct Jesus advocates is based upon the fact of a new situation, apart from which the old ways would still be valid. Even when the Church returns to the custom of fasting, the practice is reinterpreted eschatologically as a living memory of the bridegroom (v. 20). The problem of misconduct in plucking grain on the Sabbath is reduced to the clear alternative of the 'Sabbath made for man' over against 'man for the Sabbath' (2.27). But this anthropological definition of true Sabbath conduct is based in the creation intention of God, for the topic of discussion (2.27) is the purpose of God at the creation. The validity of that original purpose over against current practice is based upon the presence of the eschatological Lord of the Sabbath (2.28). The similar unclarity about 'healing on the Sabbath' (3.2) is reduced to the unambiguous alternatives of Sabbath conduct: 'do good or do evil', 'save life or kill' (3.4).[1] The reality of this distinction is then revealed in the hardness of heart of the Jewish leaders (3.5), within the sway of an evil age, and the freedom of Jesus, acting in terms of the eschatological reign of God. Thus the debates in 2.1–3.6 present an affirmation of real alternatives between right and wrong within history, and base this affirmation upon the reality of the *eschaton* within history.[2]

The subsequent debates reveal the same tendency to overcome the relativity and ambiguity of history, to set truth against error, and to champion this truth.[3]

Thus we have through a long series of debates a process of 'setting the record straight' with regard to truth, where Jesus is shown both as one who acts truly in history and one who clarifies truly the meaning of history. The eschatological basis of this understanding of history is not stated positively in these passages in terms of the nearness or dawning of God's reign.[4] However it is implicit in the negative treatment of

[1]These are the same alternatives encountered in the exorcisms; and just as 'having a withered hand' (vv. 1, 3) corresponds to 'having an unclean spirit', 'healing' (v. 2) corresponds to 'casting out', and the order 'Stretch out your hand' (v. 5) corresponds to the command 'Come out'.

[2]The eschatological orientation of the whole section (2.1–3.6) has been demonstrated by Joachim Jeremias, *Jesus als Weltvollender*, 21–32, and Harald Riesenfeld, *Jésus transfiguré*, Appendice III, 318–30.

[3]For an analysis of the antithetic structure of these debates, cf. my work *Das Geschichtsverständnis des Markus-Evangeliums*, 1956, 61 f.

[4]This point has been accentuated by Dibelius, *From Tradition to Gospel*, 222,

the Jewish tradition, which is secularized from a vantage point associated with God (7.1–23). We do not have to do with a Marcionite-like rejection of the Jewish God, but rather a rejection by the Jewish Messiah of the empirical Jewish tradition by appeal over Judaism's head to its God and scriptures. Therefore it is clear that here too the basis of argumentation is eschatological. The pattern of argumentation is to associate the Jewish authorities with the non-godly tradition of the present evil aeon, and to associate Jesus with the godly tradition of the holy history of the Old Testament, as its eschatological fulfilment. It is no accident that Jesus' allusions to Scripture tend in Mark to come from passages of 'pre-historical' intention (Eden) and 'post-historical' consummation, and from those points in the Old Testament where the divine meaning of Israel's history is particularly accentuated. With regard to divorce Jesus appeals over against legislation based upon the evil in history ('your hardness of heart' 10.5), to the true nature of human existence as it was revealed 'from the beginning of creation' (10.6). The higher authority given (10.6 f.) to Gen. 1.27; 2.24 over against Deut. 24.1 (v. 4) is not merely an arbitrary decision as to God's will, but is rather an appeal from fallen history to the situation when God's will was done on earth as it is in heaven.[1] Similarly, in the debate about paying tax to Caesar (12.13–17), the contrast between the hard fact of Caesar's dominion illustrated by the coin,[2] and the true nature of the Jewish people and of their destiny, is involved in the answer given. The distinction between the false and the true appeal to the Jewish tradition is also made by the contrast in 11.17. Here the 'den of thieves' with which Jeremiah (7.11) describes the corrupted temple which the Jewish authorities perpetuate stands over against the 'house of prayer for all nations' with which Isa. 56.7 describes the eschatological temple which Jesus brings into existence.

The issue involved in understanding correctly Jesus' teaching is the

---

in correction of the unwarranted claim to the contrary by Albertz, *Die synoptischen Streitgespräche*, 39 (cf. *Die Formeschichte des Evangeliums*, 2nd ed., 224, note 1, not translated in the Eng. ed.). Dibelius' point is to the effect that the passages had in their pre-Marcan form a didactic purpose, and were given their christological orientation only in the Marcan presentation.

[1]Lohmeyer on 10.6–8; Kümmel, 'Jesus und der jüdische Traditionsgedanke', *ZNW*, XXXIII (1934), 124; Stauffer, *TWNT* I, 647 f.; Jeremias, *Jesus als Weltvollender*, 64–69.

[2]So Klostermann; Lohmeyer; Str-B, I, 884.

'kingdom of God' (10.23, 25; 12.34), and those who have not been given the 'mystery of the kingdom of God' 'hear but do not understand' (4.11 f.). At the basis of the struggle between Jesus and the Jewish authorities is their rejection of the kingdom Jesus proclaimed (1.15) and of the 'repentance' for which that proclamation called. Therefore their attitude toward history must consist in a traditionalism which devalues the present and permits only the freedom of an interpreter of the tradition. They must be irrevocably opposed to an eschatological understanding of history which involves basic change as well as continuity, eschatological newness as well as oldness.[1] It is precisely the presence of God's reign which makes possible both the separation from frozen tradition and the deliverance from immanent relativism. God's reign is therefore the basis of Jesus' action in the Marcan debates.

### C. TEACHING AND ACTION IN MARK

The close association which has become evident between the debates and the exorcisms is simply one instance of a pervasive trend in Mark to associate the words and action of Jesus. Thus Mark gives a unity to Jesus' ministry which has often been ignored in modern presentations of Jesus.[2] Mark frequently associates the exorcisms and healings on the one hand with Jesus' teaching on the other: 'doing' and 'teaching' (6.30); 'teaching' and 'mighty works' (6.2); 'teaching' and exorcising (1.27); 'preaching' and exorcising by disciples (1.39; 3.14); 'preaching' and exorcising and healing by disciples (6.12 f.); a healing as the content of 'preaching' by the cured person (7.36). The importance of these passages is increased by the fact that a number of them occur in summaries originating with Mark.

In several of the Marcan narratives, words and action have been united because they tend to explain each other. Authoritative action confirms the authority of Jesus' word: Jesus' 'authoritative' teaching in the synagogue (1.21 f.) is clarified by the 'authority' in his word of exorcism (1.23–28); his 'authority' to forgive sin is revealed by the healing action of his word (2.1–12); the execution of the command to the fig tree (11.12–14, 20–24) surrounds the authoritative word at the cleansing of the temple (11.15–19), and this whole unit of authoritative action (cf. esp. 11.23 f.) introduces the final group of debates. It is clear

---

[1] Cf. Behm in *TWNT*, III, 451.
[2] But cf., e.g., Gerhard Kittel, *TB*, VII (1928), col. 249.

that for Mark the authority of Jesus' teaching resides not in its force of logic or the originality and profundity of its contents, but rather in the power inherent in him as Son of God and bearer of the Spirit, a power which is revealed by the efficacy of his word. When he speaks, God acts: in casting out a demon, in healing a paralytic, in forgiving sin, in addressing his people at worship. This is what cannot, according to Mark, be said of the words of the scribes (1.22). For Jesus' word is action.[1]

Even the larger blocks of Marcan teaching do not provide a haven of refuge for contemplating eternal truths apart from the cosmic struggle taking place in history. Rather the subject matter of these units is that historical struggle itself. The collection of parables has as its prelude the 'parables' of the Beelzebub debate (3.22-30, esp. 23). The interpretation of the main parable of the sower reveals that the 'word' is involved in the struggle with Satan (4.15). Mark allegorizes the parable, but not in the sense of Philo or the medieval allegories: he does not change an eschatological parable of action into moralizing eternal truths; rather he correctly interprets the parables as referring to the historical struggle and its outcome. He simply amplifies the details of that struggle beyond what was envisaged in the parable, thereby revealing his own understanding of history. This understanding is a 'mystery' which is eschatological in nature ('the kingdom of God'), and 'given' by God (4.11) through Jesus (1.15). This same understanding of the historical struggle with Satan and its outcome is the gist of the Marcan apocalypse (ch. 13). This apocalypse is not primarily concerned with speculating about the end (vv. 14-27), but rather with the struggles of the present time (vv. 5-13), the help of the Spirit (v. 11), and the exhortation to watch (vv. 28-37). It sets the frame of reference for understanding the passion narrative and the experience of the Church. The same function is performed by the only extended ethical teaching in Mark: the three discourses on suffering and humility (8.34-37; 9.33-10.31 *passim*; 10.35-45), which follow upon the three predictions of the cross (8.31; 9.31; 10.33 f.).

From the content of the Marcan teaching it is clear that the con-

[1]G. Sevenster, *De Christologie van het Nieuwe Testament*, 2. Druk, 1948, 33, cites as instances of Jesus' 'word of might': 1.25, 41; 3.5; 4.39; 5.34, 41; 7.34; 9.25. Then he makes the interesting observation that the saying can be replaced by an action: (1.41); 3.10; 5.28; 8.22. Cf. also 1.31.

fusion of men's minds is a power over man requiring divine action to be overcome (4.11): 'To you is *given* the mystery of the kingdom of God'. The Pharisaic questions are related to the 'hardness' of their hearts (3.5; 10.5). This mental confusion is also identified as Satanic temptation (8.11; 10.2; 12.15). Thus the mental problem which confronts us in the teaching of Jesus is parallel to that which in the exorcisms is due to the presence of an evil spirit or demon.

### D. THE DEBATES WITH THE DISCIPLES

Out of the three formal and parallel announcements of the passion (8.31; 9.31; 10.33 f.) there arises a type of debate with the disciples (8.32–9.1; 9.33–50; 10.35–45). Here the opposition of viewpoint is so great as to distinguish these debates from normal discussions between master and disciple, and to bring them into the present context of debates with the Jewish authorities.

The attitude of the disciples with regard to the passion had been anticipated by their failure to understand the two feedings. Here they had already been associated with the Jewish authorities (8.15). They are warned to avoid, in connexion with the feedings, the leaven of the Pharisees and of Herod. The disciples' failure to understand the meaning of the feedings is due in each case to the hardening of their hearts (6.52; 8.17), just as the Jewish authorities harden their hearts (3.5; 10.5). The disciples' lack of understanding is accentuated (6.52; 8.17, 21), and described (8.18) in Old Testament language similar to that used of the crowds (4.12; 7.18).

The attitude of the disciples with regard to the passion is introduced as Satanic (8.33), and at its culmination this attitude is put in the same context of 'temptation' (14.38) as had been the debates with the Jewish authorities. By yielding to Satan's temptation the disciples join the Jewish authorities in the cosmic struggle of Satan against Jesus which began at the temptation in the wilderness, continued in the struggle with demoniacs, advances through the historical context of these debates to right and left, and reaches its climax in the crucifixion and resurrection.

These debates with the disciples have as their main theme the effort of the disciples to dissuade Jesus from the passion, and the false understanding of discipleship which they thereby reveal. We do not have to do simply with two opposing theories of the Messiah, but rather with two understandings of eschatological existence as a whole. For the discussion of the sufferings of the Son of Man easily shifts to a debate about the rôle of the disciples in relation to the kingdom (8.34–37; 9.33–47; 10.35–44), and just as easily shifts back to witnessing to the Son of Man and his future coming in the kingdom of God (8.38–9.1), to the kingdom of God and Gehenna (9.42–50), and to the Son of Man giving his life a ransom for many (10.45).

The unity of Jesus' viewpoint in this section is in terms of the cosmic struggle, so that his teaching to the disciples is parallel to his own action, and both are in eschatological perspective. Therefore his ethical teachings are constantly parallel to christological or eschatological affirmations upon which they are modelled. Similarly the disciples are presented as consistent in their theology and ethics. The attitude which leads to Peter's theological objection to the passion (8.32), leads also to the ethically unworthy discussion among the disciples as to who is greater (9.34), to the unwillingness of the disciples to grant recognition to a new believer (9.38), to the request of James and John for places next to Jesus in his glory (10.35 ff.), and to the anger of the other ten against them (10.41). The disciples are throughout displaying the attitude due to the temptation of Satan (8.33). Thus the submission of Peter to Satan in the question of the messianic theology is carried on in the inability of Peter, James and John to ward off temptation in Gethsemane (14.38), and expresses itself in the flight of all (14.50), followed by the triple denial of Peter (14.66–72). Thus the unity of the disciples' theology, ethics, and action is maintained to the end. Their opposition to Jesus' idea of suffering corresponds to their own unwillingness to suffer, and this in turn blocks their participation in the eschatological history which Jesus awaits in Gethsemane in definitive fashion. The sharpness of the debates of Jesus with the disciples is due to the fact that the issue at stake is Mark's eschatological understanding of history, which he sees advocated and exemplified by Jesus, but opposed in word and deed by the disciples.

This survey of the Marcan material has made it clear that Mark sees the history of Jesus from an eschatological perspective. For Mark the driving force in history is the divine power of the end of time, operative already in the history of Jesus, propelling the whole course of history toward its ultimate destiny. Mark can designate this divine reality in history as the Spirit which cast Jesus into the wilderness to be tempted by Satan, and as the 'authority' (1.22, 27; 2.10; 3.15; 6.7; 11.28 f., 33) or eschatological (9.1; 12.24; 13.26; 14.62) 'power' (5.30; 6.2, 5, 14) with which Jesus carried on this struggle against the demons (1.27; 3.15; 6.7; 9.39), disease (2.10; 5.30; 6.5), and the Jewish authorities (1.22; 2.10; 11.28 f., 33; 12.24). The effect of this divine reality is Jesus' ability to maintain the struggle without attempting to break it off: on the road to Jerusalem (9.30; 10.1, 32 f., 46; 11. 1–11), in Gethsemane (14.36, 39, 41 f.), at the trial (14.61 f.; 15.2, 5), and on the cross (15.23, 30–32). This divine reality in history is the basis for both the doctrinal and the ethical correction of the disciples, and is the norm by which their conduct is evaluated. The history which Mark selects to record is presented in its unity as the eschatological action of God, prepared by John the Baptist, inaugurated at the baptism and temptation, carried on through the struggles with various forms of evil, until in his death Jesus has experienced the ultimate of historical involvement and of diabolic antagonism. In the resurrection the force of evil is conclusively broken and the power of God's reign is established in history. It is in this way that Mark understands Jesus' history. The question which still remains is as to how he understands the history in which he himself lives, subsequent to the victory of Christ, yet still among the evils of human history.

# VII

# HISTORY SINCE A.D. 30 IN MARK

## A. THE RELEVANCE OF THE QUESTION

A number of years intervene between the history Mark records and the writing of that history by Mark. In order to establish Mark's understanding of history, it is necessary to investigate his understanding of this subsequent period of 'history since A.D. 30'. For if the understanding of history which has been detected in Mark's Gospel were confined to the brief period of Jesus' public ministry, it would be unwarranted to speak in a generalizing way of that understanding as an understanding of 'history'. One would have to say that this was Mark's understanding of Jesus' history, or Mark's understanding of Jesus' biography, or Mark's understanding of Jesus. Only if it becomes clear that the understanding of history evident in the treatment of Jesus is carried over into the interpretation of other history as well, can one speak of it as Mark's understanding of history as such.

It has become clear from the study of Mark's form of presentation that he is not an objective, disinterested historian, but rather an inward participant in the history he narrates. But this does not necessarily imply that he conceives of his own time as a continuation of the kind of history which characterized Jesus' experience. Jesus' experience was for Mark not inconclusive; rather the gospel reached its dramatic climax in Jesus' vindication at the resurrection. Jesus triumphs in the struggle; is not the struggle then at an end? Certainly Jesus' struggle and his resurrection have for Mark saving significance. But this significance could be focused by Mark in either of two directions. The believer could be saved out of such a historical struggle as characterized Jesus' career; or he could be saved in that struggle, i.e., freed by Jesus' victory to continue fruitfully in the struggle on to the end, with a power and steadfast hope previously lacking to the disciples.

It is this second alternative which finds expression in such a concise statement as 10.30: 'Now in this time a hundredfold houses and brothers and sisters and mothers and children and lands, with persecutions; and in the age to come eternal life.' Mark speaks of the age to come (and the apocalyptic drama) as still future, in spite of Jesus' resurrection and the eschatological existence of the believer. This cannot be ignored as an irrelevant vestige of Jewish language. By ignoring this fact one could identify the present eschatological existence with the new aeon, and therefore describe this existence as non-historical, just as the new aeon of apocalypticism is envisaged as non-historical.[1] Mark too conceives of the new aeon in non-historical terms. But when he carefully distinguishes the existence of the Church from that non-historical aeon and defines the Church as within the present evil aeon, he is defining its existence as historical.

The non-historicity of the apocalyptic view of the new aeon

[1]This is the basic error, at least if applied to Mark, of Bultmann's tendency, 'History and Eschatology in the New Testament', 5 ff., to identify the apocalyptic view of the end of history (in distinction to the OT prophetic view of a goal of history) with the Christian understanding of the present. The apocalyptic view is stated, 7: 'History comes to an end with the ending of the old aeon. The state of welfare belongs to the new aeon, in which, according to IV Ezra 7.31, vanity vanishes, and according to Slav. Enoch 65.7, 8, times and years will be annihilated and months and days and hours will be no more.' Even if Mark envisages such a state for the 'aeon to come', he does not interpret the present in these terms. Cf. Wilhelm Michaelis' justified emphasis upon the fact that the NT does not speak of the coming aeon as having come, and his criticism of such terms as *Aeonenwende* to designate the meaning of the resurrection: 'Zur Frage der Aeonenwende', *TB*, XVIII (1939), col. 113–18. This is not to be confused with the question whether there is for Mark eschatological occurrence in the present. For Mark there certainly is; but it is eschatological occurrence in history, the 'present aeon'. Bultmann is also incorrect in citing (8) Mark 9.43, 45 on the coming 'life' as descriptions of the present, when Mark 10.29 f. makes it clear that this non-historical 'life' (Bultmann, 9, cites Mark 12.25) is not a description of the present, but of the future. Although it is true that for Mark national history has ceased to be the framework for salvation, the believer is still within history. Mark does not deny that history has meaning (Bultmann, 16: 'Henceforth history must no longer be understood as saving history, but as profane history.'); rather he repudiates a completely negative understanding of history, and achieves an understanding of history as composed of the struggle between Spirit and Satan. According to Mark's understanding of history it would not be correct to say that with the apocalyptic arrival of the new aeon history had come to an end, i.e., been repudiated; it would be more accurate to say that history would then reach its goal, the outcome of the struggle.

consisted largely in the absence of pain, suffering and evil. Suffering is however a central part of Mark's understanding of his existence. By defining the Church's existence as a combination of eschatological blessing and persecution, Mark is distinguishing it on the one hand from the non-eschatological history preceding Jesus, and on the other hand from the non-historicity of the new aeon. Mark's understanding of the Church is rooted in a new understanding of history as the inter-play of blessedness and suffering. This new understanding of history is rooted in the event in history through which a new situation in history is inaugurated. In the present chapter this thesis is to be confirmed from the various allusions in Mark to history after A.D. 30.

## B. THE TEMPORAL LIMITS OF THE MARCAN HISTORY

The Gospel of Mark covers a very brief span of time. In the debate as to the length of the public ministry of Jesus, the Marcan presenta-tion has usually been held to favour a one-year ministry. This fact has been used to question the appropriateness of designating Mark as a biography of Jesus. It raises all the more the question as to whether we have to do in Mark with a 'history'. It is at least valid to ask how far the portrayal of so brief a period can be generalized into an understanding of history as a whole.

The analysis of the Marcan introduction made it clear that the late beginning of Mark (in comparison, e.g., with the beginnings of Matt. and Luke) was intentional, and was not due to the external cause of the absence of information as to Jesus' and John's previous experience. Rather the abrupt beginning with John's preparatory baptism and the baptism of Jesus involved a relative evaluation of history prior to and subsequent to John. Mark began where he began because a new kind of history on a higher level began at that point. One cannot do justice to Mark's understanding of history by ignoring this fact. One cannot assume that what he says of Jesus' ministry was also true for him with regard to antecedent history.

The ending of Mark is unfortunately too obscure to permit of a similar analysis as to the significance of the point at which Mark drew his narrative to a close. The allusion in 16.7 to 'going before you into Galilee' (cf. 14.28) is subject to interpretations which would support each side of the debate on 'history after A.D. 30'. Lohmeyer[1] sees in the

[1]*Galiläa und Jerusalem*, 10–14.

reference an allusion to the *parousia*, so that no meaningful history would be mentioned between the resurrection and the *parousia*. On the other hand C. F. Evans[1] revives a suggestion by Hoskyns to the effect that a prediction of the gentile mission is intended, so that Mark would, like Luke, conceive of a post-resurrection history of Jesus acting through the Church. The traditional view[2] is to the effect that Mark understood the saying as referring to resurrection appearances. The statement in 16.7 is itself unclear, and the various interpretations have resorted to the general Marcan presentation for the defence of their positions. Conjectures as to the contents of a 'lost ending' of Mark cannot be made sufficiently likely to provide a basis for discussion.[3] On the other hand the ending of Mark at 16.8 is still too unproven to serve as a basis for theological deductions, which would at best be arguments from silence. Ultimately such a view would also rest upon evidence drawn from the body of Mark's Gospel rather than from the obscure ending. The most that can be said is that Mark, as we have it, covers only a brief period of time. Thus the narrow scope of the period presented by Mark does pose a problem which must be met before his understanding of history as a whole can be discussed.

In view of the distinction reflected in the Marcan introduction between history prior to John and history subsequent to John, an examination of Marcan allusions to prior history is in place. This examination will make it clear that the Marcan distinction is not the sharp rejection of Jewish history which is found, e.g., in Marcion or the Epistle of Barnabas. In the introduction Mark began deliberately with a Jewish prophet, whose appearance was itself the fulfilment of the prophecy of Isaiah. For to maintain, as Mark does maintain (specifically: 1.2; 7.6; 9.12 f.; 11.17; 12.10, 36; 14.49), that he is recording the fulfilment of Jewish prophecy, has in it a positive as well as a negative evaluation of Jewish history. That history is only

---

[1] "I Will Go Before You into Galilee," ' *JTS*, n.s., V (1954), 3 ff.
[2] Cf., e.g., J. Weiss, *The History of Primitive Christianity*, I, 14 ff.
[3] As early as B. Weiss, *Das Marcusevangelium und seine synoptischen Parallelen*, 1872, 54, the classification of resurrection appearances as beyond the Marcan concept of a Gospel raised the question as to whether Mark wrote a book of Acts later used by Luke in the first half of his Acts. Such a view was advocated by Friedrich Blass, *Philology of the Gospels*, 1898, 141 ff.; F. C. Burkitt, *Christian Beginnings*, 1924, 83; W. K. Lowther Clarke, 'The Ending of St. Mark', *Theology*, XXIX (1934), 106 f.

preliminary, in that its truth is that of prophecy. Yet as such it is preparatory, and by the fulfilment of the prophecy it receives its vindication. However it could be argued that, as in the case, e.g., of the *Epistle of Barnabas*, the prophetic value of the Old Testament could be combined with a rejection of Jewish history, on the basis that Judaism misunderstood or rejected the prophecy given to it (cf., e.g., Mark 7.6 f.; 12.2–5). The prophecy would not be envisaged as part of Jewish history, but as judgement upon Jewish history. Nevertheless it is in the person of the rejected prophet that the situation prior to Jesus is most similar to Jesus' history, and to the history of the Church. Perhaps the nearest that Mark comes to a universal in his interpretation of history is that persecution is an indispensable part of the godly life. The Jewish prophets have this in common with Jesus[1] (12.2–8); John the Baptist has it in common with Jesus (9.11–13);[2] the Christian has it in common with Jesus (10.38 f.). Therefore there is an important link connecting the two periods set apart by Mark: the persecuted witness (cf. I Thess. 2.14–16).

Furthermore Mark's use of the Old Testament is not confined to prophecy. Old Testament laws are recognized as valid (7.10; 10.7 f., 19; 12.29–33). When the Pharisees, Jews, elders, and traditions are rejected, it is by appeal to Moses (7.1 ff.); when Moses is rejected, it is by appeal to the creation narrative in the first book of Moses (10.2 ff.). Nor is Jewish history seen merely from the point of view of divine prophecy and legislation. It contains for Mark historical incidents which are exemplary, as, e.g., the incident taken from the life of the greatest Israelite king (2.25 f.). God is 'the God of Abraham and the God of Isaac and the God of Jacob' (12.26); Jesus is the 'son of David' (12.47); the coming kingdom is 'David's' (11.10); John is 'Elijah' (9.13). It is evident that the distinction which Mark makes between Jewish history and the time of Jesus is not such as to destroy all positive meaning of past history.

Once the distinction between Jesus' history and antecedent history has been clarified so as to prevent a Marcionite interpretation of that distinction, the investigation can turn to a positive definition of the difference between the two periods. When one examines Mark's under-

[1] Cf. Leonhard Goppelt, *Typos*, 1939, 92.
[2] Cf. Lightfoot, *History and Interpretation in the Gospels*, 92 f.: 'In 9.11–13 we may perhaps see the church striving to construct some kind of a philosophy of history, in the light of its convictions about the person and office of its Master, of his work and its results.'

standing of history prior to John the Baptist, it is apparent that Mark does not see there the cosmic struggle between the Spirit and Satan which he sees in Jesus' history. The baptism of Jesus with the Spirit and his temptation by Satan in the wilderness present for Mark a *novum* in history. History after this time is essentially different, on a more meaningful and intense plane than before, Mark's understanding of history cannot be reduced to a rational theory of either a moralistic or Hegelian variety. He does not mean simply that in Jesus' history the principle of all history is revealed, so that once this meaning has been learned it can be identified anywhere in any period. The Spirit comes into history upon Jesus. Similarly Jesus in preaching the nearness of the kingdom is not speaking simply of an abstract truth, namely the inescapability of God, but is referring to an event in the near future. Just as the Jewish eschatological hope envisaged a form of human existence different from historical existence as we know it (cf. the cessation of marriage 12.25), the messianic history of Jesus is conceived of by Mark as a different form of human existence from that of preceding history.

It will be the objective of the following section to demonstrate that the Marcan eschatology is such as to imply a continuation within the Church of the same kind of history as characterized Jesus' history, i.e., a struggle between Spirit and Satan, until the final outcome of that struggle is reached and the goal of history attained. However, assuming such an outcome of the following investigation, a further question remains with regard to the Marcan distinction of history B.C. and A.D. To what extent can an understanding of history which applies only to the Christian era, and perhaps only to those parts of history in the Christian era where the Church is present, be envisaged as an understanding of history as such, and not merely an understanding of Christian history, or of Church history? Apparently Mark would not use the 'understanding of history' evident in his Gospel for treating the history of earlier times or other cultures. In this sense his understanding of history is not intended as a tool for the scholarly historian. But it is at this point that one must recall that although Mark himself can be called a 'historian' in the sense that he is a writer of historical occurrences and their meaning, he is himself not a scholarly historian, in terms of research and objectivity. His book is not a 'document' or a 'source', but rather a 'witness', a 'Gospel'. It is not intended as enlightenment for the scholar as scholar, but rather as guidance for man as man. The understanding of history which Mark provides is the understanding of history which applies to each reader of his Gospel. As a key to the historical experience of the reader, Mark's understanding of history is universal. That is to say: As an interpretation of history written and read in the Christian era and by those within the Church or who encounter the Church, it is of validity for every reader who is attempting to understand the history in which he finds himself. This existential form of universality which characterizes Mark's understanding of history is rooted in the fact that Mark envisages the cosmic struggle as extending to all peoples and continuing to the culmination of history. Mark's understanding of history shares in the universality of the cosmic struggle itself.

## C. THE MARCAN APOCALYPSE

Although we must for the purposes of discussion assume that Mark's Gospel terminated with the resurrection, we are not left completely without references to the future. As a matter of fact, the book characterizes itself as eschatologically orientated by the quantity of references to the future event bringing history to its consummation. This event is envisaged by Mark as a future event in time and space (cf. 13.32; 'day and hour'; 13.33: 'the time'). It is now generally recognized that the kingdom which Jesus preached was envisaged primarily as future, with its present activity as the exception to or as the anticipation of the future completeness. The distinctiveness of the future coming is particularly accentuated in 9.1 by the description of that coming as 'in power'. Through the association with the immediately preceding verse (8.38), this coming of the kingdom is identified with a coming of the Son of Man, which is also distinguished from Jesus' present coming by the characterization: 'in the glory of his father with the holy angels'. Similarly the distinctiveness of the future coming of the Son of Man is described (13.26): 'in clouds with much power and glory'. Only with this event does the radical transformation take place (13.27). Therefore descriptions which are of a clearly non-historical nature[1] must be placed after that event. It is the

[1] 12.25: 'When they rise from the dead, they neither marry nor are given in marriage, but are like angels in heaven'; 13.31; 'heaven and earth will pass away'; 9.43–47: 'life' (43, 45) or 'the kingdom of God' (47) as the alternative to 'gehenna'; 10.30: 'eternal life' as characteristic of 'the coming age' in distinction from now in 'this time'.

central importance of this final future event as a fixed point on the horizon which gives to the outlook of Mark a horizontality, a temporality, which distinguishes Mark from the mystery religions, which tend to direct attention inward or upward, out of time into eternity. The fact of the future event produces the attitude of alertness with regard to the events of time and space which finds expression in the repeated admonitions to 'watch' (13.34, 35, 37), 'take heed' (13.5, 9, 23, 33), 'stay awake' (13.33). The future event is but the completion of the eschatological history of Jesus which Mark has recorded, as is evident from the continuity of the concepts of the kingdom and of the Son of Man from Jesus' history to the *parousia*. This tends to give the intervening period its orientation (cf., e.g., 2.20), and to suggest the interpretation of that period in terms of the struggle with which it begins and the final victory with which it terminates. It is this suggestion which finds its confirmation in the Marcan apocalypse.

The modern history of the interpretation of the Marcan apocalypse[1] has revolved around two inescapable facts: (1) The Marcan apocalypse at times clings to the language of prophecy, providing a more visible identification in the history of Jewish apocalyptic language than in the course of historical events. (2) The Marcan apocalypse at times fits the events of first century history and of the book of Acts so completely that it seems to be history written in the form of a *vaticinium ex eventu*. Unfortunately the significance of this tension for the understanding of Mark has been largely lost in the debate as to whether the Marcan apocalypse is a real prophecy (whence the stereotyped language and its historical vagueness), or is actually a *vaticinium ex eventu* (whence its historical clarity), or is perhaps a combination of the two (whence the tension). Irrespective of the way in which the origin of the Marcan apocalypse be explained, the tension itself exists, and must be interpreted as such in an interpretation of Mark.

1. On the one hand we have to do with history written in the form of *prophecy*. The Church is specifically exhorted (13.23) to find the meaning of its historical experience in terms of the fact: 'I have told you all things beforehand.' It is therefore no accident that the history of the Church is present in the form of a prophecy. History which occurs according to prophecy is history with God-given meaning. To call upon the Church to interpret its history as prophesied is to call upon

---

[1]This history is thoroughly presented by G. R. Beasley-Murray, *Jesus and the Future*, 1954.

the Church to interpret its history theologically. Furthermore it is of considerable relevance for Mark that the prophecy comes from Jesus: the history of the Church proceeds from, is given by, Jesus. This is the significance of the fact that motifs in the apocalypse are often echoes of important passages from the narrative concerning Jesus.[1] It is clear that the experiences of the Church are presented in the Marcan apocalypse as prophesied by and modelled after the history of Jesus.

2. The other aspect of the tension in the Marcan apocalypse is the fact that the prophecy has to do with events of *history*. The fact that Mark sees his life lifted up into a theological dimension by the redemptive action of the heavenly Lord does not eliminate the fact that this theologically understood life is seen as historical experience. When Matthew and Luke accentuate the historicity of the narrative more than does Mark,[2] they are only continuing a trend already present in Mark. For Mark provides both temporal sequence (13.7, 8, 10, 14, 21, 24, 26, 27) and language descriptive of present history (13.9 ff.).[3] The experience of the Church depicted in the apocalypse involves such matters of

[1]Parallels have been drawn to the Marcan parables (3.20–4.34) by Lightfoot, *The Gospel Message of St. Mark*, 40; Farrer, *A Study in St. Mark*, 164–6; to the three predictions of the passion and the subsequent definitions of discipleship (chs. 8–10) by Busch, *Zum Verständnis der synoptischen Eschatologie*, 39 ff.; and to the passion narrative esp. by Lohmeyer, 'Die Reinigung des Tempels', *TB*, XX (1941), 257–64, summarized by Lightfoot, *The Gospel Message of St. Mark*, 48–59. For further parallels see below.

[2]Matthew, e.g., by adding temporal terms so as to heighten the sense of sequence (24.9, 10, 14, 29), Luke by using language which points to historical facts such as the fall of Jerusalem (21.20–24).

[3]Günther Harder, 'Das eschatologische Geschichtsbild der sogenannten kleinen Apokalypse Markus 13', *Theologia Viatorum* IV (1952), 71–107, distinguished sharply between Mark's and Luke's 'view of history'. Luke gives an 'interpretation [of Mark 13.14–20] from contemporary history' (91), and in general 'engages in an eschatological interpretation of history', i.e., his presentation is 'determined by contemporary events and their prophetic interpretation in the Church' (101). Mark sees the destruction of the temple 'precisely not as a political event, but as an occurrence which goes beyond the dimensions of the historical and therefore as eschatological' (103), a drama set off by the death and resurrection of Jesus (102). But Harder's sharp distinction breaks down on his concession (98) that Mark's 'subject-matter' is 'the historical event of the expansion of the Christian Church and her conflict with synagogue and State government'. Nor is it accurate from Mark's point of view to speak of his presentation as 'exceeding the dimensions of the historical', since Mark's understanding of history is throughout

public and official nature as courtroom proceedings (13.9, 11), international wars (13.7 f.), and messianic pretenders (13.5 f., 21 f.).[1] The Church is seen as involved in experiences which are historical in nature, although these historical experiences are prophesied by Jesus, interpreted in the light of his experience, and seen as a commentary upon the exhortation to take up one's cross and follow him. The Christian is called upon to understand his history, not just his mystic or cultic experience, in the same way as he understands the history of Jesus. The statement (13.11) that the Holy Spirit will guide Christians in their defence before hostile courts is merely a confirmation of the fact which is already evident, that the struggle between the Spirit and Satan continues in the history of the Church.

### D. THE CHURCH OF JEWS AND GENTILES

The fact that the Marcan Apocalypse presents events of Church history in the form of a prophecy from Jesus provides the key for interpreting the aspects of Jesus' history which also have a *Sitz im Leben* in Church history. Previous scholarship has found primarily two ways of explaining such parallels. The cult relived in a mystic way experiences of Jesus' history; or the apologetic pragmatism involved in the Church's struggle for existence (viewed from a completely immanent point of view) led to basing various customs of the Church in incidents of Jesus' life. Neither of these solutions takes account of Mark's eschatological understanding of history, which sees Jesus and the Church engaged in the same cosmic struggle against the same demonic force of evil.

---

eschatological, as Harder himself emphasizes (99). To be sure, if Harder means here by the 'historical' a modern definition such as the 'non-miraculous', then Mark exceeds the 'historical'—but then so also does the whole NT. The sharpness of Harder's antithesis between Mark and Luke is also blunted by the concession that Mark 13.10 'stands near to the Lucan conception' (104 f.), and that Luke 21.34-36 is 'a fragment of the older [Mark] eschatological view of history' (97). Cf. Conzelmann, *Die Mitte der Zeit*, 108. But even as Harder's antithesis stands, it does not correspond to the Bultmannian antithesis between Paul and Luke. For Harder maintains that both Mark and Luke have eschatological views of history and he presents Luke's as largely dependent on Rom. 11.25 (101). Harder's presentation contains little which could not be explained by the fact (presupposed 104) that Mark wrote before, and Luke after, the destruction of Jerusalem.

[1]Cf. further Busch, *Zum Verständnis der synoptischen Eschatologie*, 62.

It would denote a secularizing modernization in one's understanding of the early Church, to assume that its appeal to Jesus in explaining its action was a *post facto* procedure brought on only by the opposition the Church encountered. Rather the action of the Church was motivated by its faith, and opposition was inherently awaited from such action. When then the Church appeals to Jesus in its debates, it is merely bringing into the open the understanding of its action latent in its faith.

If on the other hand the eucharist and other 'cult legends' were the only part of the life of the Church which Mark traced back to scenes in the life of Jesus, one could argue that the history of the Church (in distinction from its cultic mysteries) was not necessarily understood in terms of Jesus' history. But the missionary activity of the Church is traced back to the lifetime and initiative of Jesus (3.13 ff.; 6.7 ff., 30). This missionary activity of the disciples in Mark, consisting of voyages, hardships, healings, exorcisms, and witnessing (the same ingredients as compose the history of Jesus), must be described as historical experiences. This can be particularly illustrated by the fact that one historical event of great world-historical importance is likewise rooted by Mark in the history of Jesus: the success of the gentile mission.

The shift of Christianity from Palestine and a Jewish membership to the whole Mediterranean world and an inter-racial membership is a well established fact in the history of the period between Jesus' life and the time when Mark wrote his Gospel. The impact of this historical fact[1] upon Mark is not only obvious from indications suggesting that he himself lived outside Palestine,[2] but also from the importance of gentiles and non-Jewish territory in his Gospel (esp. chs. 6–8). The necessity, e.g., of explaining (7.3 f.). a Jewish custom to the reader and the way in which this explanation is stated ('For the Pharisees and all the Jews . . .') indicate that Mark does not understand himself and his reader as falling within Judaism, either theologically or culturally. The discussion with the Syrophoenician woman (7.24–30) can only be understood in terms of a historical process envisaged on the pattern 'first the Jews and then the gentiles', a pattern whose

[1]G. H. Boobyer, 'Galilee and Galileans in St. Mark's Gospel', *BJRL*, XXV (1952–3), 340, lists as 'possible allusions' to the gentile mission: 1.17; 4.23; 10.45; 11.17; 14.24; and as 'definite' allusions: 12.9; 13.10, 27; 14.9.
[2]Cf. B. W. Bacon, *Is Mark a Roman Gospel?* 1919.

existence in the early Church is thoroughly documented in Paul and Luke-Acts.

The rejection of Jewish custom (7.1 ff.) can only be understood correctly when one realizes that Mark rejects gentile custom in equally categorical terms (10.42). It is clear that we do not have to do in Mark with some racial or national preference, but rather with some third viewpoint from which all past custom can be rejected. The evidence can best be explained in terms of the Christian's eschatological awareness of being distinct from the historical custom of the present evil aeon, whereby it becomes irrelevant whether that custom be Jewish or gentile. The association of the gentiles with the Jews in the guilt for executing Jesus[1] is to be understood in terms of the classification of the whole generation to which Jesus came as the present evil aeon.[2] Similarly Paul associates both Jew and gentile in guilt under the law (Rom. 1–3), or under the στοιχεῖα (Col. 3.8, 20; Gal. 4.3), so that all the executioners of Jesus can be brought together as under the sway of 'the rulers of this age' (I Cor. 2.8). The same association of Jews and gentiles is also envisaged by Mark in the persecution of Christians (13.9), a further indication of the correspondence which exists between his theological understanding of Jesus' history and of the Church's history. Both Jesus and the Church bear the Spirit within the present evil aeon, and consequently suffer at its hands.

It is clear that the presence of gentiles in the Church is understood theologically by Mark. They are really no longer 'gentiles', but Christians. Yet within this theological appraisal is included the historical fact that the gentiles have since the history of Jesus entered into the Church in such proportions as to put them alongside the Jews in the saving significance and prophetic meaning of the history of Jesus. This would seem to be the suggestion of the two feedings, in so far as the numbers 12 and 7 are given special prominence (8.19 f.) and may be associated with the communion of the Jews and gentiles (cf. e.g., Acts 6.1 ff.).[3] There are also indications that Mark sees in the

---

[1]Mark is noticeably more reticent in exonerating Pilate than are Matt. (27.19, 22, 24 f.) and Luke (23.4, 20, 22, 25).

[2]Cf. 8.12, 38; 9.19; 13.30 and Büchsel, *TWNT*, I, 661.

[3]Cf. G. H. Boobyer, 'The Miracles of the Loaves and the Gentiles in St. Mark's Gospel', *SJT*, VI (1953), 80 ff. Cf. also Lightfoot, *History and Interpretation in the Gospels*, 182–205.

death of Jesus a particular significance for the admission of the gentiles.[1]

The various traces within Mark of a pattern of history including as an important aspect the entrance of the gentiles into the Church are brought together into a unified presentation by the parable of the wicked tenants (12.1–11). The introduction of the vineyard theme in the language of Isa. 5.2 makes it clear that the parable's vineyard is, from the first verse on, understood as the people of God. In the Marcan parable the Jewish people—either as a whole or in the person of their leaders—have repeatedly rejected God's servants, until by rejecting his Son they are themselves rejected.[2] Thus they lose the 'inheritance' they sought (v. 7), and it is turned over to 'others' (v. 9). These 'others' are obviously the Christians, and while it would be too much to say that a Church composed only of gentiles is intended,[3] to say the least this understanding of the Church presupposes the rejection of the Jews and thus by implication the inclusion of the gentiles. Furthermore the course of the parable has for Mark the significance of a sketch of history, so that it confirms the pattern of the course of history which has already been sensed in Mark and which is everywhere presupposed in his understanding of the nature of history: There is the time of the prophets, followed by the time of Jesus, which is followed by the time of the Church. The former two times have in common for Mark a prophetic significance, but are separated by the point at which the fulfilment begins; the latter two times have in common for him the struggle of the Spirit *versus* Satan, but are separated by the point at which the decisive victory takes place.

The result of this investigation into Marcan history after A.D. 30 is

---

[1]This interpretation of Jesus' passion is presented by Lightfoot, *The Gospel Message of St. Mark*, 60–69, and by C. F. Evans, ' "I will Go Before You into Galilee",' *JTS* n.s., V (1954), 15. Further bibliography is listed by G. H. Boobyer, 'The Miracles of the Loaves and the Gentiles in St. Mark's Gospel', *SJT*, VI (1953), 83, n. 1. Cf. esp. M. Kiddle, 'The Death of Jesus and the Admission of the Gentiles in St. Mark', *JTS*, XXXV (1934), 45 ff.

[2]Mark 4.10–25 may also be the reflection of Mark's awareness of the rejection of the Jews. The passage is in tone parallel to Rom. 9–11, and, in view of the Marcan parable of the vineyard, may reasonably be associated with the theological problem posed by the general failure of the Jewish mission. So Lightfoot, *History and Interpretation in the Gospels*, 76.

[3]With Jülicher, *Die Gleichnisreden Jesus*, II, 403 f.; Goppelt, *Typos*, 92 f.; Kümmel, 'Das Gleichnis von den bösen Weingartnern', *Aux sources de la tradition chrétienne*, 1950, 128.

that history since the resurrection is conceived of as a continuation of the same cosmic struggle which Jesus began. While this conclusion cannot be used as a proof of such conjectures as a Marcan Church history following 16.8, yet the results attained in the present study should be sufficient to stop exaggerated statements as to the impropriety of Luke's writing the book of Acts, as well as to put in question the antithesis between history and Christianity upon which such criticisms are based.

# VIII

# HISTORICAL ÀTTITUDE AND COMMUNAL HISTORY

In the study of 'history since A.D. 30' it has become evident that Mark understood the history of his own time and experience in the same way as he understood the history of Jesus. In the present chapter this conclusion should receive its confirmation and application. For here the question is to be raised as to the historicity of Mark's own religious outlook, and as to the nearest historical milieu in which he finds himself. The first question is directed to his definition of 'piety', indicating the direction of what could perhaps be called a Marcan 'psychology of religion'. The second question is directed to Mark's definition of 'Church', indicating the direction of what could perhaps be called a Marcan 'sociology of religion'. This study of his 'stance' toward his own history and of his 'construction' of that history should provide the 'subjective' and 'objective' statements of his own relation to history.

The method for investigating Mark's own religious attitude is based upon the following considerations. The Jesus of the story Mark tells is the heavenly Lord he worships. In the course of the story various personages assume differing attitudes towards Jesus. As Mark evaluates these attitudes, he reveals his own attitude. By establishing the attitude which is for Mark normative, one can establish Mark's own norm of piety.

## A. THE NUMINOUS IN MARK

Expressions of the numinous[1] feeling are undoubtedly frequent in Mark. These numinous expressions have been identified as the central Marcan concept of piety by those who have attempted to prove the

---

[1]For the definition of this term and the philosophy of religion which it represents, cf. the classic formulation by Rudolf Otto, *The Idea of the Holy*, 2nd ed., 1950. He cites (158) Mark 10.32 as the formulation of this feeling toward Jesus.

appropriateness of the conclusion at 16.8, a verse containing four numinous expressions.[1] The reaction of scholarship against the historicizing interpretation of the nineteenth century with its low Marcan christology led to an accentuation of the high christology of Mark, which would well correspond with a numinous definition of piety.[2] However the present analysis has served to show that the loftiness of Jesus, although unquestioned by Mark, is not central in his presentation, which is rather concerned with Jesus' struggle, action and suffering. The Marcan Jesus is not *of* history, but on the other hand he is not aloof from history; rather he comes, gives himself into the historical situation, and performs a history-creating function. Therefore the numinous definition of piety is not necessitated by the Marcan view of Jesus.

In 10.32 the disciples follow Jesus to Jerusalem in awe and terror. The basic difficulty in identifying this verse as the centre of Mark's ideal of piety is that this scene falls within the section of debates between Jesus and the disciples about suffering. The attitude of the disciples in 10.32 is parallel to Peter's rebuke to Jesus (8.32), the disciples' discussion as to who is greatest (9.34), their amazement at the difficulty of salvation (10.24, 26), the request of James and John for places of prestige (10.35, 37), and the indignation of the other ten (10.41). The interest in glory and greatness reflected in this attitude is rejected by Jesus, just as the cowardly fear here so closely associated with this attitude is opposed to the conduct of Jesus.

The nearest parallels to 10.32 in its combination of cowardly fear and numinous awe on the part of the disciples are the two scenes on the sea (4.40 f.; 6.49–52). Both stories begin with cowardly fear and conclude with numinous awe. The intimate association of the two attitudes is evident from the fact that the verb φοβεῖσθαι refers in 4.41 to awe (as in 5.15; 16.8; perhaps 6.20; 9.32), while in 6.50 ('do not fear') it refers to cowardice (as in 5.33, 36; 11.18, 32; 12.12; perhaps 6.20; 9.32). Furthermore both attitudes are attributed to unclarity as to Jesus; fear is due to lack of faith (4.40), confusing Jesus with a ghost

[1] Cf. especially Lindton, 'Der vermisste Markusschluss', *TB*, VIII (1929), col. 229–43.

[2] The interpretation of Ebeling, *Das Messiasgeheimnis und die Botschaft des Marcus-Evangelisten*, brings this implication of the work of Wrede to the forefront. Otto, *The Idea of the Holy*, 159, has rightly seen in the numinous feeling toward Jesus the beginning of the high christology of later centuries.

(6.49), and not knowing that 'it is I' (6.50); awe expresses itself with the question 'Who is he?' (4.41), and is explained (6.52) as follows: 'for they did not understand about the loaves, but their heart was hardened'. (Could Mark add such a commentary to his ideal of piety?) Fear and awe are not here distinguished as one would distinguish non-Christian and Christian attitudes to Jesus, but both are brought together and stand over against the Christian confession of Jesus as Son of God (15.39).

It is true that the first Marcan expression of amazement toward Jesus (1.22, 27) is presented uncritically as a testimony to Jesus. But when Mark comes to a thematic discussion of admiring designations of Jesus (6.14–16; 8.28), it is clear that they do not have his approval. Even the title Messiah must be corrected from its pompous Jewish to its humble Christian meaning (8.29–33). Therefore the synagogue scene (1.23–27) received in Mark a limitation which it may not have had in its oral circulation, and must find its commentary in its nearest Marcan parallel, the synagogue scene of 6.1–6. The amazement of 1.27 is repeated in 6.2; but this amazement is then expounded as offence (v. 3), dishonour (v. 4), an obstacle to the divine action (v. 5), lack of faith (v. 6). Jesus amazes those who know him according to the flesh (v. 3a); but Mark knows him according to the Spirit.

One could expect Mark to attribute his ideal of piety to Jesus, and to withhold it from Jesus' enemies. His usage with regard to fear and awe is just the reverse. In only two instances is such an attitude attributed to Jesus: in his home town when his power fails and he is amazed at their lack of faith (6.5 f.), and in Gethsemane where he is 'amazed and disturbed' (14.33). These are precisely the two passages in Mark where Jesus falls out of his normal rôle as bearer of the Spirit, and stands—like the disciples (cf., e.g., 9.18; 14.38, 50)—over against God, and separated from his eschatological *dynamis* (6.5; 14.36). It is obvious that it was not this attitude of awe which brought forth the history of Jesus which Mark records.

On the other hand both cowardly fear and numinous awe characterize the authorities opposed to Jesus: They 'fear' the crowd (11.32; 12.12), and even 'fear' Jesus (11.18). They do not 'dare' question Jesus further (12.34; contrast 15.43). This 'fear' shifts imperceptibly into 'amazement' with numinous overtones at Jesus' answer to their question as to tax for Caesar (12.17). But such awe does not prevent these authorities from putting Jesus to death, any more than Herod's numinous 'fear' of John (6.20) prevented him from executing John, or Pilate's 'amazement' at Jesus (15.5, 44) prevented the execution. Mark doubtless appreciated the awe in which Jesus was held by his enemies, just as he appreciated the confessions of the demons. But just as the demons were none the less silenced and cast out, the enemies of Jesus remain none the less his enemies. It is therefore inconceivable that an attitude which is applied to Jesus only inconsistently, but which characterizes those who put him to death, could be regarded by Mark as the ideal of piety.

Mark's rejection of awe as a religious ideal may be due to the effect it has of suspending the action of Jesus, and thus of blocking the eschatological history Mark advocates and records. Overawed in the presence of the numen, man shrinks back (5.33). This fear must be overcome before action is possible (5.36). However a numen is not only awesome, but also fascinating,[1] and Mark's Jesus creates not only awe and fear, but also excitement, attention, crowds. If Mark is interested in the historicity of Jesus, it could be this quality of fascination, bringing Jesus to the attention of the authorities and thus into world history, which was of interest to him.

Jesus' great popularity finds expression primarily in the chorus-like reactions on the part of the crowd. This motif has been identified[2] as a stylistic convention of the Hellenistic world for accentuating the completeness of the cure or the greatness of the healer. When one inquires as to Mark's appraisal of this aspect of the material before him, one first observes that in most cases he makes no comment upon the motif, leaving it with its implicit positive significance: 1.22, 27; 2.12; 5.20, 42; 7.37; 11.18; 12.37; etc. However when one investigates Mark's designations of those who give expression to this attitude of fascination, it becomes increasingly difficult to find in them his ideal of piety.

The groups expressing such mass acclaim are not clearly defined, but are variously designated as those in the 'synagogue' (1.21, 23, 29; 6.2), or 'all' (1.27; 2.12; 5.20), or the 'crowd' (11.18; 12.37), or simply

---

[1] Cf. Otto, *The Idea of the Holy*, 31.

[2] Cf. Bultmann, *Die Geschichte der synoptischen Tradition*, 241. Cf. also Lindton, 'Der vermisste Markusschluss', col. 231. The Marcan list given by Bultmann and Lindton could be supplemented by the following passages: 5.15, 20, 33; 6.2; 11.18; 12.37.

'they' (7.37; 5.42).[1] These and other designations for the chorus do not indicate that Mark looked with favour on this group. The 'synagogue' is Jesus' habitual place for teaching (1.39; 3.1). Yet it is also the scene of persecutions to Christians (13.9), and the site of the scribes' pride (12.39). The 'crowd' of 4.1 is defined (v. 11) as 'those outside' in distinction from the 'twelve', and the 'crowd' is taught in riddles so that they will not understand and repent (v. 12; cf. also 7.14, 18). The 'crowd' presses Jesus (3.9; 5.24, 31), prevents him from eating (3.20), obstructs his contact with those he wishes to help (2.4; 5.31). The 'crowd' is hardly for Mark the chosen people, for when it is defined geographically in terms of Jewish-inhabited areas of Galilee (3.7 f.), it is the group from which Jesus retires to choose the twelve.[2] 'Israel' occurs in Mark only incidentally, in quoting the Shema (12.29), and in the taunt 'Christ King of Israel', in which scene the taunting Jewish authorities are hardly for Mark the holy people of God. Jerusalem is the source of 'crowds' (3.7 f.), but this city is itself appraised as the source of opposition (3.22; 7.1), and is subject to Isaiah's condemnation (7.6 f.). It is the city putting Jesus to death (10.32, 33; 11.1, 11, 15, 27; 15.41), whose temple awaits destruction (13.2) and desecration (13.14).[3] The Marcan term for 'crowd' is a secular term (ὄχλος), while he avoids the term λαός, which is rendered sacred in the LXX as the designation of the chosen people. The latter term is rare in Mark (con-

---

[1] Mark makes no distinction between 'all' and 'the crowd'; in 2.4 the same group is called 'the crowd' which in 2.12 is called 'all'; cf. 9.15: 'all the crowd'. When there is no specific subject ('they'), the same vague chorus is sometimes intended, apparently without further reflection: 7.37 refers to the crowd of v. 33; similarly the parallel passage 5.42 may refer to the 'tumult' (v. 39) of 'all' (v. 40), rather than to the intimate circle actually present.

[2] Lohmeyer, *Galiläa und Jerusalem*, 26–36, avoids this antithesis between the twelve and what he assumes to be a definition of Galilee by saying that the calling of the twelve 'strengthens' the Church Jesus has founded in Galilee. Apart from the fact that this verse supports the small definition of Galilee rather than Lohmeyer's large boundary, the whole section presents Jesus as avoiding the crowd (3.7, 9, 13), not strengthening the Church. The way in which Lohmeyer avoids the other negative attitudes toward Galilee in Mark (6.1–6), and reads an emphasis upon Galilee into positive Marcan contexts (mission of the twelve; Peter's confession; the transfiguration) is equally artificial. Lohmeyer assumes *a priori* that Jesus' audiences are holy, but this logic is refuted in 2.13–17. Cf. also John 1.5, 11. Lohmeyer's embarrassment with the Marcan material is evident in his creation of a 'Galilean secret' corresponding to the messianic secret.

[3] Cf. Lohmeyer, *Galiläa und Jerusalem*, 29, 33–34.

trast Matt. and Luke), occurring in the LXX usage only in a quotation *in malam partem* against the Pharisees and scribes as 'hypocrites' (7.5 f.), and in the secular sense in 14.2.[1] To this absence of positive designations for the chorus there corresponds a series of negative characterizations: 'the many who are coming and going' (6.31); 'those who are weeping and wailing' (5.38); 'this adulterous and sinful generation' (8.38);[2] 'unbelieving generation' (9.19).[3] The fascinated crowds who surround Jesus are clearly not looked upon with favour by Mark.'

One must conclude that Mark's norm of piety is not to be found in the concept of the numinous, in either its awesome or its fascinating aspect. If the one attitude is insufficient because it tends to separate Jesus from history, the other tends to confuse him with history, so that Jesus himself withdraws from the mass scenes (1.35; 3.9, 13; 4.1, 35; 5.40; 6.31, 45; 7.33; 8.13; 9.2, 28, 30). Thus Mark's reservations with regard to the numinous correspond to the limits of his understanding of history: eschatology, Jesus and the Spirit are not aloof from history, but rather enter history and create history; but they are not immanent forces which develop out of the present evil aeon as its potentiality. Rather, they must 'come' from heaven at a certain time and place, not as the perfection of the present evil aeon, but as the beginning of its end.

## B.  FAITH AND UNDERSTANDING

If one is to take seriously Mark's specific exhortations 'not to fear' (5.36; 6.50; 16.6; cf. also 13.7), then one must look to his accompanying positive statements for his preference in religious attitudes. 'Cowardice' is contrasted with 'faith' during the storm (4.40). Jairus on hearing of his daughter's death is admonished; 'do not fear, just

---

[1]Cf. Strathmann, *TWNT*, IV, 49–52.

[2]Cf. Hauck, *TWNT*, IV, 742, and Büchsel, *TWNT*, I, 661. The odd introduction of the 'crowd' v. 34 may find in this allusion its explanation.

[3]This designation refers less to the disciples, whose faith is not in question, than to the father, 'one of the crowd' (v. 17) whose presence had been emphasized vv. 14 f. For it is the father's faith which is the subject of discussion (vv. 23 f.) For the eschatological significance of this term cf. Str-B I, 641; IV: 2, 976 ff. Volz, *Die Eschatologie der jüdischen Gemeinde im neutestamentilchen Zeitalter*, 1934, 148, shows how this eschatological designation can be used of a historical situation.

believe' (5.36; cf. also vv. 33 f.). The 'astonishment' of Jesus' home town (6.2) is identified as 'disbelief' (6.6), just as the 'amazed' crowd of 9.15 is an 'unbelieving' generation (v. 19). It is obvious that 'faith' is one term which Mark chooses to designate the religious attitude preferable to that of awe. Similarly the 'amazement' at Jesus' walking on the water (6.50 f.) is explained: 'for they did not understand', for 'their hearts were hardened' (6.52). At the transfiguration Peter's inappropriate suggestion is explained: 'for he did not know what to say, for they were terrified' (9.6). In 9.32 'they did not understand the saying, and were afraid to ask him'. It is the same situation as 10.24, 26, where the disciples are 'amazed', but are unclear as to Jesus' teaching and ignorant as to how to be 'saved', whereas the 'faith' of the sick woman and of Bartimaeus 'saved' them (5.34; 10.52). It is clear that 'understanding' is closely associated with 'faith' in defining the religious attitude Mark advocates. Therefore an analysis of these two interrelated terms should provide a clarification of Mark's ideal of piety.

The importance of the attitude of 'faith' for Mark is evident from the fact that it is the attitude which Jesus calls forth and praises. Jesus reproaches 'disbelief' (4.40; 6.6; 9.19), exhorts to 'faith' (5.36;11.22), and goes out of his way to attribute praiseworthy action to 'faith' (2.5; 5.34; 10.52).

When one asks what meaning the term 'faith' bears for Mark, one is first struck by the intimate association between 'faith' and the eschatological action constituting the Marcan history. The woman's act of touching Jesus' garments is an act of faith, and is welcomed as such by Jesus (5.34); the attitude of awe accompanied her misgivings (v. 33), and, if dominant, would have prevented the action altogether. Therefore as the interrupted story of Jairus is resumed, Jairus is exhorted to 'faith' rather than 'fear' (v. 36), so that the action of Jesus can continue in spite of the apparent death of the daughter. The association of 'faith' and Jesus' action is negatively accentuated in his home town, where he can hardly perform any 'mighty deeds' because of their 'unbelief' (6.5 f.). The importance of the attitude of 'faith' is such as to attribute to it, rather than to Jesus, the cure, 2.5; 5.34; 10.52. Similarly in 9.23 the issue is shifted from Jesus to the faith of the epileptic's father, so that the power is attached to the faith: 'Everything is possible to him who believes' (9.23). This power of faith to bring about the action of God is discussed thematically after the withering of the fig tree (11.22–24).[1]

Mark's interpretation of the attitude of 'faith' does not consist simply in its relation to action, but includes also a relation to knowing. The verb is transitive and the noun has a referential aspect: 'Faith' is 'in the gospel' (1.15) or 'in God' (11.22). One 'believes that what one says will happen', or 'that you received', and believing corresponds to praying (11.23 f.). 'Believing' also corresponds to saying that John the Baptist is 'from heaven' (11.31). It is an act of recognition, to be denied to false Messiahs (13.21), but which would be granted to Jesus as 'Christ King of Israel' if he would come down from the cross (15.32). Those who are 'Christ's' are called 'believers' (9.41 f.), so that 'believer' becomes a Christian self-designation presupposing some profession of Jesus as Christ. From this survey it is clear that Mark has no single person or act as the object of faith, and no specific credal statement as the content of faith.[2] Rather it is faith in the action recorded in the Marcan history, irrespective of whether the language refers to God causing the action, Jesus as able to perform it, the gospel proclaiming it, or prayer calling for it. Therefore while faith as action leads to the synonym 'take courage' (6.50; 10.49), faith as knowing leads to the synonym 'follow'. This is such a typical description of the disciples' attitude (1.18; 2.14 f.; 3.7; 5.24; 6.1; 10.52; 14.54; 15.41) that it becomes a technical designation of the disciples (10.32; cf. 9.38), and takes on symbolic theological significance (10.21, 28, 32, 52; 14.54; cf. also 8.34). It never loses its concrete relation to the history of Jesus, but is reserved by the early Church for those who 'followed' him during his earthly life.[3]

The aspect of 'knowing' which inheres in Mark's interpretation of

[1]This power of faith cannot, from Mark's point of view, be psychologized as the therapeutic value of confidence. Those whose faith is discussed are sometimes (2.5; 9.19, 23 f.) not the invalids themselves. The few miracles Jesus does in spite of unbelief are such as would, from the psychological viewpoint, require faith (6.5 f.), while the primary discussion of wonder-working faith (11.22–24) is treating not of healings open to psychological interpretation, but rather of miracles in the world of nature. In 2.5 faith effects the forgiveness of sins, not the cure.

[2]Cf. Martin Werner, *Der Einfluss paulinischer Theologie im Markusevangelium*, 106–18, where Mark's view of faith is distinguished from Paul's theologically fixed concept of 'faith in Christ'.

[3]Cf. Kittel in *TWNT*, I, 214.

'faith' recalls its close association to the term 'understanding'. When one investigates the Marcan usage of the latter term it becomes evident that it does not fall outside the scope of the term 'faith', not does it even shift the Marcan ideal of piety away from the action aspect to the knowing aspect of 'faith'. Rather 'understanding' holds a centre of balance between the two aspects of 'faith'.

There are in Mark two things which are not 'understood': the feedings (6.52; 8.17, 21) and the parables (4.12; 7.14). In neither of these cases is it really a matter of comprehending intellectually a doctrine. The feedings are actions, not teachings (the incidental instructions *are* understood), and misunderstanding reveals itself in a kind of action; amazement at Jesus walking on the water (6.51), and concern about bread in the boat (8.14, 16). This action is a confused reaction to Jesus, failing to recognize in him—through the feedings—the action of God in history. In the parables too the problem of understanding is not intellectual, but existential: the 'parable' of what defiles (7.17) calls for 'understanding' (7.14, 18), but the interpretation consists less in adding any new insight to the discussion of vv. 1–14 than in pressing home a conclusion ('cleansing all foods' v. 19) which was difficult for some to accept. Similarly the 'parable' of the fig tree (13.28) is more an exhortation than an instruction, and the interpretation (v. 29), in view of its vagueness, serves more as a concluding exhortation than as a clarification of details. Two parables are apparently understood intellectually (3.23; 12.1, 12) but repudiated existentially, so that the hearers are rejected (3.29; 12.12).

If Mark does not associate the problem of 'understanding' with that of intellectual clarification, he does associate it with the problem of 'hardness of heart' (6.52; 8.17).[1] This agrees with Mark's general view that the opponents of Jesus suffer from 'hardness of heart' (3.5; 10.5). Thus the problem of 'understanding' is removed from either an intellectual or a psychological context, and is endowed with the theological overtones which accompany the idea of 'hardness of heart' in the Old Testament history of God's people.[2]

[1]This term does not occur with regard to the parables, but its equivalent OT expression used in 8.18 of the feedings occurs in 4.12 of the parables: 'seeing they see and do not know, and hearing they hear and do not understand.' In the OT context (Isa. 6.9 f.), reference is made specifically to hardening (lit. 'fattening') of the heart (cf. Matt.).

[2]Cf. K. L. and M. A. Schmidt, *TWNT*, V, 1024–32.

The thematic discussion of the problem of 'understanding' takes place in terms of a discussion of understanding parables (ch. 4). The first and longest parable is intended to explain the problem of understanding 'parables' as such (4.10–13): 'You do not know this parable, and how will you know all the parables?' The chapter as a whole is concerned with two levels of 'hearing': one is 'hearing but not understanding' (4.12); the other is the 'hearing' for which the chapter repeatedly calls (vv. 3, 9, 23, 24; cf. 7.14). This motif of two levels of understanding finds expression also in the repeated withdrawal from the 'outsiders' (4.11) to privacy for the interpretation (vv. 10, 33 f.; cf. 7.17). The interpretation of the first parable (vv. 14–20) is devoted to an explanation of these two levels: the superficial level, called 'seeing' and 'hearing' (v. 12), is exemplified by those who 'hear' the word but then fall away (vv. 15, 16, 18). The deeper level, called 'knowing' and 'understanding' (v. 12), is itself the objective of the interpretation (v. 13), and is exemplified by the fourth example: 'These hear the word and receive it and bear fruit thirtyfold and sixtyfold and a hundredfold' (v. 20). Most illuminating are Mark's explanations for the two levels: progress from the first to the second level is blocked by the cosmic enemy of Christ, Satan (v. 15). His action is explained as 'tribulation and persecution on account of the word' (v. 17), 'the cares of the age and the deceitfulness of riches and the desires for the rest' (v. 19). The deeper level is given by God (v. 11),[1] and corresponds to the 'repentance' and 'forgiveness' (v. 12) for which the gospel calls (repentance: 1.4, 15; 6.12; forgiveness: 1.4; 2.5, 7, 9, 10; 3.28 f.; 11.25). Thus the struggle for 'understanding' is the inner aspect of the eschatological struggle between Satan and God constituting the history of Jesus.

When Jesus gives understanding to those 'who have eyes but do not see and ears but do not hear' (8.18; cf. 4.9, 12, 23 f.), he is engaged in the same activity as when he gives sight to the blind (8.22–26; 10.46–52) and hearing to the deaf (7.32–37; 9.14–29): 'He has done all things well; he even makes the deaf hear and the dumb speak' (7.37). Herein is confirmed the unity between the whole Marcan presentation of Jesus' history on the one hand and his evaluation of the attitude of 'faith' and 'understanding' on the other. It is therefore evident that we have identified Mark's ideal of piety. This ideal is an attitude orientated

[1]The passive form implies God as the agent. Cf. Jeremias, *The Parables of Jesus*, 12, 15.

in terms of the eschatological struggle and committed to the historical action of Jesus and the Spirit. Mark does not advocate a non-historical, mystical religiosity, but rather gives expression to a religious attitude which recognizes the historicity of human existence.

## C. THE SOCIETY CREATED BY JESUS' ACTION

Mark's understanding of history has been characterized as an awareness of two history-making forces in conflict with each other. Therefore the action of the Spirit in Jesus and the Church is an aspect of history moving toward its goal, just as the régime of the present evil aeon is an aspect of history moving toward its end. Correspondingly Mark's religious attitude is one of historical commitment. However, the sporadic vertical actions of the Spirit and the alertness of the believer to his historicity do not fully justify the assertion that one has to do in Mark with Jesus' and the Church's *history*. For the term 'history' normally contains a sociological factor; it is the movement of a society or people. This brings with it traditions and custom, and in the long run a culture. If Mark conceived of Jesus immanently, as a continuation of the present evil aeon, the sociological impact of Jesus' history would be submerged within first-century Judaism. If Mark conceived of Jesus' action as purely transcendent, anti-historical, one would not expect a sociological factor, but at most a cluster of individual ascetics. If however Mark does look upon Jesus and the Church as both eschatological and historical, one would expect to find indications of a historical society, with its customs, ethos and tradition. However, such objectified manifestations of a history, such a movement toward the universal, toward status, toward empirical evidence, stand in a certain tension with the spirituality of the forces at work in history. They are in tension with the non-objectivity of Mark's presentation of Jesus' history, and to the risk and existential commitment involved in a religious attitude of historicity. If in spite of this tension Mark proceeds to include such a sociological dimension in his presentation, this must be evaluated as a confirmation of his intention to present a *history* of Jesus (and the Church), as well as a definition of piety.

The oral material about Jesus came to Mark bearing two traits of primary significance for the problem of Jesus and society: the material was in disconnected units, and it represented Jesus as leading an itinerant way of life. These motifs are used by Mark to present the origin of an eschatological society. Mark makes the first feeble beginnings toward temporal and geographic connexion of the stories.[1] But he also exploits the absence of a geographic connexion to accentuate that Jesus comes from God.[2] The 'comings' of Jesus in 1.24, 38; 2.17; 10.45 far surpass in significance the antecedent geographic 'comings' of 1.21, 35; 2.13; 10.1, and take on (esp. 11.11) the eschatological significance of 'coming' (8.38; 9.1, 11, 12, 13; 10.30; 11.9 f.; 13.6, 26, 35–6; 14.62; 15.36). Similarly in Jesus' itinerant way of life ('passing by': 1.16, 19; 2.14) he calls upon people to 'follow' him (1.17, 20; 2.14) in a two-fold sense (1.17b, 20; 2.17). Thus a recurrent motif of the historical narration is that he is 'followed': by many tax-gatherers and sinners (2.15); by a multitude (3.7); by a crowd (5.24); by disciples (6.1); by women (15.41). Mark makes it clear that this 'following' assures an eschatological restoration in this age and eternal life in the age to come (10.28–31; cf. vv. 17, 21), i.e., entrance into the kingdom of God (10.23). Thus Jesus separates persons from their natural and historical setting, and introduces them into an eschatological existence of communion with himself.

This eschatological existence is not, however, a private relationship to Christ, but is an existence shared with a group of disciples. The follower is separated from one society and placed in another. This society is on the one hand the inevitable travel companionship of the itinerant way of life, and on the other hand a theologically understood relationship. They are 'the twelve', suggestive of the twelve tribes of Israel,[3] a title to which Mark draws specific attention only in the listing of the names (3.16–19). They are 'apostles' (i.e., 'emissaries' 6.30), but only in connexion with their mission (3.14; 6.7). Their function is primarily for Mark 'so that they could be with him' (3.14). Jesus is 'with the twelve' (11.11; 14.17), or the inner group (9.8; 14.67; cf., also 1.29), or the unidentified disciples (2.19; 3.7; 4.36; 8.10). Thus a technical term for discipleship arises: 'those with him' (5.40; perhaps 1.36); 'those going up with him' (15.41); to 'be with him' (5.18). The theological significance of this term is also evident from its frequency

---

[1] Cf. K. L. Schmidt, *Der Rahmen der Geschichte Jesu.*

[2] Already Schweitzer, *The Quest of the Historical Jesus,* pointed to the 'positive non-connexion' of the narratives, which he correctly interpreted as suggesting some 'supernatural' or 'dogmatic' meaning (334 f. of the 1950 edition).

[3] Cf. Rengstorf, *TWNT,* II, 325 f.

in the communion of the last evening (14.14, 17, 18, 20, 33), which is shattered by Judas 'with a crowd' (v. 43) and Peter 'with the guards' (v. 54), denying that he had been 'with the Nazarene Jesus' (v. 67).

Although the number and designation of those 'with Jesus' varies, this group is clearly distinguished from the crowd by Mark. They are distinguished from the crowd terminologically (2.15; 3.9; 5.31; 6.45; 8.34; 9.14; 10.46), or by special functions (3.9; 6.35, 41; 8.1, 6; 11.1), authority (9.38; 10.13), power (3.15; 6, 7, 12 f.; cf. also 9.18), or customs (2.18; 7.2 f.). A recurring motif is that Jesus withdraws from the crowd to be with the disciples (3.7–19; 6.31 f.). Usually this withdrawal is for the sake of special instruction, whose significance is thus accentuated: 4.10, 34; 7.17; 9.28, 33–35; 10.10, 32; 13.3. Therefore this society is the bearer of certain esoteric teaching (cf. also 10.23; 11.14). What 'men' say of Jesus is distinguished from what 'you' the disciples say (8.27 ff.), for the disciples possess the messianic secret. They also witness certain important events (1.29; 5.37; 9.2), especially in passion week (11.11; 14.17, 33). They observe the scene (14.3–9) which is to be reported 'wherever the gospel is preached into all the world'. They are instructed as to Jesus' death (8.31; 9.31; 10.32) and resurrection (9.9; 10.33; 16.7). Thus the new society is identified as the bearer of the *kerygma*.[1]

It is clear that this society is understood theologically by Mark. Its members are those to whom the eschatological redeemer has come. He has removed them from a worldly society and incorporated them into an eschatological society. As witness to Jesus' eschatological history, this society is defined as 'Christ's' (9.41).

## D. THE ESCHATOLOGICAL COMMUNITY

Two of the points at which Jesus' followers were most rudely snatched from their historical settings by their eschatological faith were their family relationships and their table fellowships. Here the early Christian could sense quite existentially the reality of being dehistoricized. Yet it is precisely here that Mark makes it clear that the history which has been lost is replaced by a new history.

[1]The rôle of the twelve in Mark is not such as to prove the existence of a 'twelve-source', as has been maintained by Eduard Meyer, *Ursprung und Anfänge des Christentums*, I, 135 ff. Cf. the critique by C. H. Turner, 'Marcan Usage: Notes, Critical and Exegetical, on the Second Gospel. VIII. "The Disciples" and "the Twelve",' *JTS*, XXVIII (1926–7), 22–30.

Jesus had to break with his own family (3.19b–21, 31–35; 6.1–6). James and John forsook their father Zebedee (1.20), and the departure from Capernaum (1.36) took Peter and Andrew from their home (1.29–31). Such a disruption of family ties will characterize the end (13.12), when 'brother will betray brother to death and the father his son, and children will rise against their parents and have them put to death'. The new aeon will have no marriage (12.25). When the rich man is called upon to sell his property and follow Jesus in order to have 'eternal life' or the 'kingdom of God' (10.17, 21, 23–26), the latent theological significance of this sacrifice bursts into the open: Peter had 'left all' to 'follow' Jesus (10.28); it was for Jesus' sake and the gospel's (v. 29).

This leads to the thematic discussion of the eschatological replacement for the loss (10.30). The replacement is not simply the non-historical existence of the (still future) aeon to come, but first of all a new society: 'a hundredfold houses and brothers and sisters and mothers and children and fields'. The historicity of this society is accentuated by locating it 'now in this time' (i.e., within the present evil aeon). All that is listed as lost in one society (v. 29) is regained in the other a hundredfold.[1] Similarly the lists of Jesus' spiritual family (3.34 f.) are equally extensive with the lists of his natural family (3.31 f.); 'mother and brothers'; 'brother and sister and mother'. Therefore we do not have to do with an ultimate break with society, but only with the question (3.33) as to 'who is my mother and brothers'. This new society conforms to Mark's understanding of the history of the interim as a struggle: over against the blessings stands the promise of 'persecutions' (10.30).[2]

[1]The omission of the father is intentional in the same way as is that omission in the remarkably complete listing of Jesus' natural (3.31 f.; 6.3) and spiritual (3.33–35) family. God is the father of Jesus (8.38; 14.36) and Jesus is his son ([1.1]; 1.11; 3.11; 5.7; 9.7; 12.6; 14.61; 15.39), so that the two bear these titles absolutely (13.32). But Jesus speaks to the disciples of 'your father which is in heaven' (11.25), so that the gap in both Jesus' and the Christian's spiritual family is filled by God himself.

[2]If the general Jewish outlook was more historical than the Greek, by the fact that the Jew envisaged a goal of history, the Christian was even more historical, by the fact that this goal is itself historical during the interim. This verse avoids both the pessimism latent in the Greek view of history and the naïve utopianism and self-glorification latent in the Jewish view. Cf. the criticisms of this verse (cited by Taylor, *Comm.*) by the Greek-thinking Clement of Alexandria and Julian the Apostate, and by the Jewish-thinking chiliasts.

The replacement of the natural family by the spiritual family is not in itself the non-historical existence 'like the angels', where 'they neither marry nor are given in marriage' (12.25). Rather Christian existence includes the monogamy of the garden of Eden (10.6). Jesus defends the integrity of the home (7.10–13; 10.2–12), yields to the requests of parents for their children (5.21 ff.; 7.24 ff.; 9.14 ff.), accepts the parents' faith for the cure of the children (5.36; 7.28; 9.24; cf. 1.31), grants to the parents the privileges of disciples (5.40), and sends cured persons home (2.11; 5.19; 8.26). Blood relationships among Christians are not ignored: 1.16, 19; 3.17; 5.37; 15.21, 40. However these relationships are relativized in terms of new Christian relationships; Peter has been separated from Andrew and associated with James and John (3.16–18; 5.37; 9.2; 13.3; 14.33);[1] James and John become 'sons of thunder' (3.17);[2] for the twelve apostles themselves replace the twelve patriarchs and make possible the interracial Marcan Church. The natural society is not an absolute, but must be reformed in terms of the spiritual society. In this sense the Christian family is for Mark a historical reality which has become eschatological. It can serve as a norm not for destroying other history, but for restoring it and directing it toward its goal.

Table fellowship is the other place where Mark shows a clear awareness of the separation from one history, society, custom and culture, and the entrance into another history, which also has its customs, society and ethical principles.

Mark's presentation of table fellowship is particularly useful in interpreting his understanding of his own history, since these passages reveal more clearly than most their *Sitz im Leben* in the early Church. The fact that table fellowship presented various problems for the early Church is evident from such passages as Gal. 2; I Cor. 8–11; Acts 6. The discussion of fasting (2.19 f.) refers specifically to the time of the Church. The debate concerning purification before meals (7.1 ff.) is clearly presented from the Christian, not from a Jewish context (v. 3). The last supper (14.22–25) is obviously the Church's eucharist (cf. I Cor. 11.23–26). The request of James and John (10.35–45), in view

[1]The order in 1.29 is an exception required by the narrative: 'into the house of Simon and Andrew with James and John.'

[2]Their blood relationship is emphasized precisely where it becomes a harmful factor (10.35).

of its eucharistic motifs (sitting beside Jesus; drinking his cup; serving; his life a ransom for many), may reflect eucharistic difficulties such as those of I Cor. 11.27–34. But also the two feedings of the multitude (6.34–44; 8.1–9, 14–21) are eucharistic.[1] Therefore it is evident that Mark's presentation of table fellowship reflects his understanding of his own situation.

Mark's table fellowship is for him a sacred, eschatological society. The eucharist is the fellowship of the interim, looking back upon Jesus' death (14.22–24; 10.38 f. 45), and forward to the *parousia* (14.25). It is the communion of the eschatological 'covenant' (14.24). Jesus feeds his Church miraculously and superabundantly (6.34 ff.; 8.1 ff.), and the 'Son of Man' feeds his disciples as the Lord of the eschatological Sabbath (2.23–28).[2] Just as feasting is in the presence of the eschatological bridegroom, fasting is in terms of his absence (2.19 f.). Therefore it is evident that this table fellowship is not a secular or peripheral part of Mark's experience, but rather a sphere where the eschatological reality is the formative factor.

Now it is this eschatological table fellowship which displays most clearly the concomitant trappings of historical reality. It has its own customs: Its Sabbath practices are different from the Jewish tradition (2.23 ff.; 3.1 ff.), and in the first instance with regard to eating. It has its own fasting customs, outwardly parallel to Judaism, but understood in a new way (2.18–20; 14.25), and perhaps observed on a different day.[3]

---

[1]Pfleiderer, *Primitive Christianity*, II, 25 ff., points to the eucharistic feeding of the multitude in John 6.51–58; the five loaves and two fishes of early eucharistic paintings; the function of the deacons in the love-feast as described by Justin Martyr; the evening hour, at the close of the discourse, with the people reclining in orderly ranks and companies; and the eucharistic language in the blessing on the bread. Riesenfeld, *Jésus transfiguré*, 321, has shown that this last parallel is not coincidental, by illustrating how the similar wording of Mark 2.26 (and Luke 6.4) departs from that of I Kgdm., 21.6 (LXX) in the direction of the eucharistic phraseology. The absence of the cup does not argue against this interpretation, but rather recalls the 'breaking of bread' of Acts 2.42, 46; 6.1–6 (cf. Lohmeyer, 'Das Abendmahl in der Urgemeinde', *JBL*, LVI [1937], 228 ff.). Compare also the meals of the Qumran sect, in the *Manual of Discipline*.

[2]Cf. Lohmeyer, 'Vom urchristlichen Abendmahl', *TR*, n.F., IX (1937), 203.

[3]The phrase 'on that day' may allude to Friday as the day of Christ's death, in contrast to the Monday and Thursday fasts of the stricter Pharisees (cf. Luke 18.12; *Didache* 9.1). So Holtzmann, *Die Synoptiker*, 3. Aufl.; Gulin, *Die Freude im Neuen Testament*, 2, n. 1; Lohmeyer (*Comm.*); Klostermann (*Comm.*), with doubts. Lagrange (*Comm.*) holds that the allusion is too vague.

It has the custom of eating with unwashed hands, while the Jews observe the tradition of ceremonial cleansing before meals (7.2–5). This is cited as merely one point at which the Christian custom no longer follows the Jewish tradition (7.4).

Some of the instances where Christian custom varies from Jewish custom are of ethical significance; Jewish divorce regulations are rejected (10.2–12). The Corban subterfuge is rejected (7.9–13). The immoral scribal way of life, including its mealtime customs, is rejected (12.38–40). Similarly the gentile custom of 'lording it over' inferiors is rejected, and here too within the context of the Christian table communion, where 'service' is the ideal (10.42–45; cf. 9.35). The terms 'serve' and 'servant' retain their two-fold significance of waiting on tables (1.13, 31; 15.41) and of ethical service (10.45).[1] 'Compassion' predominates at the two miraculous feedings (6.34; 8.2; cf. 5.43; 9.41). Therefore the rejection of immoral custom leads to new ethical custom. For the Christian is not left to the *ad hoc* guidance of the Spirit for his ethical conduct, but is supplied with a warning *Lasterkatalog* such as was current in the Jewish and Hellenistic cultures of the day: 'evil thoughts, fornication, theft, murder, adultery, coveting, wickedness, deceit, licentiousness, an evil eye, slander, pride, foolishness' (7.21 f.)—as well as with the ten commandments (10.18 f.). These general ethical maxims are significant not only because their observance makes communal life possible, but also because the existence of generally valid ethical principles gives to the Marcan ethic a cultural in addition to its existential aspect.

The Marcan table fellowship is also involved in the correct definition of its constituency. Its policy of inclusiveness is attested on all sides: it admits 'tax-gatherers and sinners' (2.13 ff.); the eucharist is for the 'many' (14.24; 10.45);[2] the Syrophoenician woman is after all 'fed' (7.25–30).[3] The emphasis upon 'the children's crumbs' (7.28) has as its parallel the emphasis in both miraculous feedings on the quantity of

[1]Cf. Beyer, *TWNT*, II, 92.

[2]J. Jeremias, *The Eucharistic Words of Jesus*, 123–5, demonstrates that 'many' accentuates inclusiveness, not exclusiveness, and that this inclusiveness envisages specifically the gentiles (146–52). Cf. also Lohmeyer, 'Das Abendmahl in der Urgemeinde', *JBL*, LVI (1937), 227.

[3]The delay seems to reflect the pattern 'first the Jew and then the Greek', which is the flag under which the Pauline inclusiveness could be carried through (Rom. 1.16; 2.9 f.; Matt. 10.5 f.; 28.19; Acts 1.8).

broken pieces left over (6.43; 8.8). This aspect of the two feedings is brought forward as what is to be 'understood' (8.14–21).[1] The miracle of the multiplied food points to the miracle of the Church, that the eschatological reality is sufficiently inexhaustible to make possible a society open to all humanity.

It has become clear that Mark sees eschatological existence in terms of the life of a society which is sufficiently historical to have assumed already in Mark's time some of the cultural and traditional aspects of a historical organism. This society has its ethos, its *mores*, its constituency. Furthermore, each of these is for Mark rooted in the history of Jesus, and envisaged in eschatological perspective. This is not to say that these more mundane aspects of historical existence are central in Mark's understanding of history; but they do indicate that Mark's understanding of Christian existence consists in an understanding of history: the history of Jesus and the history of the Church.

[1] The association between the Syrophoenician's 'crumbs' and these 'broken pieces' is accentuated by the fact that these two passages correspond to each other in the doublet: 6.34–7. 23 and 8.1–26. Cf. the chart by Klostermann, *Comm.* Other associations between the feedings and the inclusion of gentiles have been observed; the twelve baskets for the twelve apostles, and seven for the hellenistic deacons (Acts 6.1–6; so Lohmeyer, 'Das Abendmahl in der Urgemeinde', *JBL*, LVI [1937], 235 ff.; cf. also Klostermann, *Comm.*); the inclusion of the doublet so as to represent the tradition of the two branches of the Church (so Sundwall, *Die Zusammensetzung des Markusevangeliums*, 50); the location in the Decapolis (cf. G. H. Boobyer, 'The Miracles of the Loaves and the Gentiles in St. Mark's Gospel', *SJT*, VI [1953], 78 ff.).

# AUTHORS

Albertz, M., 91, 92, 96 n.

Bacon, B. W., 112 n.
Barth, K., 61 n., 64, 67 n.
Bauer, W., 88 n., 93 n.
Bauernfeind, O., 84, 86
Beasley-Murray, G. R., 109 n.
Behm, J., 97
Beyer, H. W., 132 n.
Blass, F., 105 n.
Blass-Debrunner, 70 n.
Bonner, C., 88 n., 93 n.
Boobyer, G. H., 112 n., 113 n.,
    114 n., 133 n.
Büchsel, F., 88 n., 113 n., 121 n.
Bultmann, R., 58 n., 59 n., 62 n.,
    64 f., 65 n., 66, 66 n., 67 n., 91,
    92, 103 n., 111 n., 119 n.
Burkitt, F. C., 105 n.
Busch, F., 110 n., 111 n.

Calvin, J., 62 n.
Campbell, J. Y., 72 n.
Carrington, P., 59 f.
Clark, K., 72 n.
Clarke, W. K. Lowther, 105 n.
Conzelmann, H., 67 n., 70 n.

Deissmann, A., 85 n., 88
Dibelius, M., 61 n., 73 n., 90 n.,
    91, 92, 96 n.
Dodd, C. H., 72 n., 80 n.
Drews, A., 58

Ebeling, H. J., 56 n., 62 f., 91 n.,
    117 n.
Erbt, W., 58
Evans, C. F., 105

Farrer, A., 60, 110 n.

Foerster, W., 88 n.
Fuchs, E., 64, 66 n.
Fuller, R. H., 72 n.

Goppelt, L., 106 n.
Grant, F. C., 59 n.
Grundmann, W., 79 n.
Gulin, E. G., 71 n.

Harder, G., 110 f., n.
v. Harnack, A., 66 f., n.
Hauck, F., 121 n.
v. Hofmann, J. Ch. K., 72 n.
Holtzmann, H. J., 56 n., 131 n.
Hoskyns, E., 105

Jeremias, J., 95 n., 96 n., 125 n.,
    132 n.
Jülicher, A., 114 n.

Kähler, M., 57 n.
Käsemann, E., 62 n., 64 n., 67 n.
Kierkegaard, S., 63
Kittel, G., 97, 114 n., 123 n.
Klostermann, E., 70 n., 79 n.,
    96 n., 131 n., 133 n.
Kraeling, C. H., 73 n.
Kümmel, W. G., 59 n., 63 n., 72 n.

Lachmann, C., 55 n., 70 n.
Lagrange, M. J., 131 n.
Lake, K., 88
Lightfoot, R. H., 59, 59 n., 70 n.,
    73 n., 78 n., 106 n., 110 n.,
    113 n., 114 n.
Lindton, O., 117 n., 119 n.
Lohmeyer, E., 59 f., n., 63 n.,
    70 n., 73 n., 77 n., 88 n., 96 n.,
    104, 110 n., 120 n., 131 n.,
    132 n., 133 n.

Messel, N., 76 n., 94 n.
Meyer, E., 128 n.
Michaelis, W., 103 n.
Morgenthaler, R., 72 n.

Nestle, E., 70

Oepke, A., 59 n.
Oldshausen, H., 72 n.
Ott, H., 65 n.
Otto, R., 78 n., 116 n., 117 n., 119 n.
Overbeck, F., 66 f., n.

Pfleiderer, O., 131 n.
Procksch, O., 84 n.

Raschke, H., 58
Rawlinson, A. E. J., 59 n.
Rengstorf, K. H., 127
Riesenfeld, H., 95 n., 131 n.
Ritschl, A., 56
Robinson, J. M., 80 n., 95

Schmidt, K. L., 60 f., 62 n., 64 n.,
    67 n., 73 n., 124 n., 127 n.
Schmidt, M. A., 124 n.
Schniewind, J., 61, 70 n.
Schweitzer, A., 56 n., 57, 127 n.

Schweizer, E., 77 n.
Sevenster, G., 98
Stauffer, E., 88 n., 96 n.
Strack-Billerbeck, 73 n., 88 n.,
    96 n., 121 n.
Strathmann, H., 121 n.
Strauss, D. F., 55 n.
Sundwall, J., 133 n.

Taylor, V., 70 n., 129 n.
Troeltsch, E., 64 n.
Turner, C. H., 128 n.

Volkmar, G., 59
Volz, P., 121 n.

Weber, F., 94 n.
Weiss, B., 105 n.
Weiss, J., 105 n.
Weisse, C. H., 56 n.
Wellhausen, J., 57, 58 n., 71 n.
Wendland, H. D., 79
Werner, M., 59, 123 n.
Westcott-Hort, 70
Wilke, C. G., 55 n.
Windisch, H., 73 n.
Wrede, W., 57, 59 n., 62, 83 n.,
    86 n., 117 n.

# BIBLICAL REFERENCES

| Bible Ref. | Page |
|---|---|
| *Genesis* | |
| 1.27 | 96 |
| 2.24 | 96 |
| *Deuteronomy* | |
| 24.1 | 96 |
| 24.4 | 96 |
| *I Sam* (I Kngd. LXX) | |
| 21.6 | 131 n. |
| *II Kings* | |
| 1.8 | 73 |
| *Isaiah* | |
| 5.2 | 114 |
| 6.9 f. | 124 n. |
| 49.24 ff. | 78 |
| 49.25 | 79 n. |
| 56.7 | 96 |
| *Daniel* | |
| 12.1 | 76 |
| *Micah* | |
| 3.8 | 77 n. |
| *Matthew* | |
| 4.17 | 69 |
| 10.5 f. | 132 n. |
| 11.7 | 73 |
| 11.9–14 | 70 |
| 11.11a, 12 | 80 n. |
| 11.18 | 73 |
| 12.27 | 86 |
| 20.8 | 70 n. |
| 21.20–24 | 110 n. |
| 21.32 | 80 n. |
| 24.9 | 110 n. |
| 24.10 | 110 n. |
| 24.14 | 110 n. |
| 24.29 | 110 n. |
| 27.19 | 113 n. |
| 27.22 | 113 n. |
| 27.24 f. | 113 n. |
| 28.19 | 132 n. |
| *Mark* | |
| 1.1 | 71, 80, 129 n. |
| 1.1–13 | 70 |
| 1.2 | 72, 105 |

| Bible Ref. | Page |
|---|---|
| *Mark* | |
| 1.2–3 | 72 |
| 1.2–8 | 72 |
| 1.3 | 73 |
| 1.4 | 69, 71, 73, 125 |
| 1.4–8 | 72 f., 75 |
| 1.4–13 | 72 |
| 1.5 | 70, 73 f. |
| 1.6 | 73 |
| 1.7 | 74 |
| 1.7, 8 | 75 |
| 1.7–13 | 76 |
| 1.8 | 70 n., 74, 76, 83 |
| 1.8–12 | 77 n. |
| 1.9 | 70, 74 |
| 1.9–12 | 74 |
| 1.9–13 | 69, 74, 75 |
| 1.10 | 74, 76 |
| 1.10–12 | 85 |
| 1.11 | 129 n. |
| 1.12 | 76, 77 |
| 1.13 | 132 |
| 1.14 | 69, 70f., 73, 79 |
| 1.14 f. | 69, 71, 78, 79 |
| 1.14 ff. | 70 |
| 1.15 | 72, 78 n., 79, 80, 97, 98, 123, 125 |
| 1.16 | 127, 130 |
| 1.17 | 112 n., 127 |
| 1.17 f. | 127 |
| 1.18 | 123 |
| 1.19 | 127, 130 |
| 1.20 | .27, 128 |
| 1.21 | ⸱19 |
| 1.21–28 | 82, 127 |
| 1.22 | 92, 98, 101, 118, 119 |
| 1.23 | 82, 83, 84, 119 |
| 1.23–26 | 92 |
| 1.23–27 | 88 |
| 1.23–28 | 97 |
| 1.24 | 83, 84, 85, 86, 127 |
| 1.25 | 84, 86, 88, 98 |
| 1.26 | 83 n. 86, 87 |

| Bible Ref. Mark | Page | Bible Ref. Mark | Page |
|---|---|---|---|
| 1.26 f. | 84 | 2.28 | 95 |
| 1.27 | 83 n., 84, 92, 97, 101, 118, 119 | 3.1 | 95 n., 120, 131 |
| | | 3.2 | 93, 95 |
| 1.29 | 119, 127, 128, 130 | 3.2–5 | 92 |
| 1.29–31 | 129 | 3.3a | 118 |
| 1.31 | 89, 98 n., 130, 132 | 3.3 | 95 n., 118, 125 |
| 1.32–34 | 82 | 3.4 | 95, 118 |
| 1.34 | 77 n., 83 n., 86, 88 | 3.5 | 89, 95, 98 n., 99, 118, 125 |
| 1.35 | 121, 127 | | |
| 1.36 | 127 | 3.6 | 118 |
| 1.38 | 85 n., 127 | 3.7 | 120 n., 123, 127 |
| 1.39 | 82, 83 n. 86, 88, 97, 120 | 3.7 f. | 120 |
| | | 3.7–12 | 82 |
| 1.41 | 98 n. | 3.7–19 | 128 |
| 1.43 | 88 | 3.9 | 120, 121, 125, 128 |
| 1.44 | 89 | 3.10 | 98 n. |
| 2.1–12 | 97 | 3.10, 11 | 82 |
| 2.1–3.6 | 94, 95 | 3.11 | 83, 84, 85, 86, 92, 129 n. |
| 2.4 | 120 | 3.11 f. | 86 |
| 2.5 | 122, 123 n., 125 | 3.12 | 84, 88 |
| 2.6 f. | 93 | 3.13 | 118 n., 121 |
| 2.6–11 | 92 | 3.13 ff. | 112 |
| 2.7 | 94, 125 | 3.14 | 97, 127 |
| 2.10 | 94, 101, 125 | 3.15 | 77 n., 83 n., 86, 88, 101, 128 |
| 2.11 | 90, 130 | | |
| 2.11 f. | 89 | 3.16–18 | 128 |
| 2.12 | 119, 120 n. | 3.16–19 | 127 |
| 2.13 | 127 | 3.17 | 130 |
| 2.13 ff. | 132 | 3.19b–21 | 129 |
| 2.13–17 | 120 n. | 3.20 | 120 |
| 2.14 | 127 | 3.21–30 | 78 |
| 2.14 f. | 123 | 3.22 | 83 n., 120 |
| 2.15 | 127, 128 | 3.22 f. | 77, 86, 88 |
| 2.16 | 93 | 3.22 ff. | 81, 82, 86 |
| 2.16 f. | 92, 94 | 3.22–30 | 83, 84, 92, 98 |
| 2.17 | 85 n., 127 | 3.23 | 84, 124 |
| 2.18 | 73, 118 | 3.24 | 84, 124 |
| 2.18–20 | 131 | 3.25 | 84 |
| 2.18–22 | 92 | 3.26 | 84 |
| 2.19 | 94, 127 | 3.27 | 78, 79, 80, 84, 86, 88 |
| 2.19 f. | 130, 131 | 3.28 f. | 125 |
| 2.20 | 95, 109 | 3.29 | 84, 124 |
| 2.21 | 95 | 3.29 f. | 77, 84 |
| 2.22 | 95 | 3.30 | 83 n. |
| 2.23 ff. | 131 | 3.31 f. | 129 |
| 2.23–28 | 131 | 3.31–35 | 129 |
| 2.24–28 | 92 | 3.33 | 129 |
| 2.25 | 106 | 3.34 f. | 129 |
| 2.26 | 131 n. | ch. 4 | 125 |
| 2.27 | 95 | 4.1 | 120, 121 |

| Bible Ref. Mark | Page |
| --- | --- |
| 4.9 | 125 |
| 4.10 | 128 |
| 4.10–13 | 125 |
| 4.10–25 | 114 n. |
| 4.11 | 98, 99, 120, 124, 125 |
| 4.11 f. | 96 |
| 4.12 | 99, 120, 123, 124 n., 125 |
| 4.13 | 125 |
| 4.14 | 125 |
| 4.15 | 98, 125 |
| 4.16 | 125 |
| 4.17 | 125 |
| 4.18 | 125 |
| 4.19 | 125 |
| 4.20 | 125 |
| 4.23 | 112 n., 125 |
| 4.34 | 128 |
| 4.35 | 121 |
| 4.36 | 127 |
| 4.37 f. | 89 |
| 4.39 | 86 n., 88, 89, 98 n. |
| 4.40 | 117, 121, 122 |
| 4.40 f. | 117 |
| 4.41 | 117, 118 |
| 5.2 | 83 |
| 5.2 f. | 88 |
| 5.3–5 | 87 |
| 5.5 | 86, 88 |
| 5.6 | 85 |
| 5.6–13 | 92 |
| 5.7 | 83, 84, 85, 129 n. |
| 5.8 | 83 n., 84, 86 |
| 5.9–13 | 84 |
| 5.10–12 | 86 |
| 5.13 | 83 n., 87 |
| 5.14 | 101 |
| 5.14–20 | 82 |
| 5.15 | 87, 117, 119 n. |
| 5.15 ff. | 84 |
| 5.18 | 127 |
| 5.19 | 88, 90, 130 |
| 5.19 f. | 82 |
| 5.20 | 119 |
| 5.21 | 130 |
| 5.21 ff. | 130 |
| 5.24 | 120, 123, 127 |
| 5.28 | 98 n. |
| 5.30 | 101 |
| 5.31 | 120, 128 |

| Bible Ref. Mark | Page |
| --- | --- |
| 5.33 | 117, 118, 119 n., 122 |
| 5.34 | 89, 98 n., 122 |
| 5.36 | 117, 118, 121, 122, 130 |
| 5.37 | 128, 130 |
| 5.40 | 121, 127, 130 |
| 5.41 | 98 n. |
| 5.41 f. | 87 |
| 5.42 | 119, 120 |
| 5.43 | 86 n., 89, 132 |
| ch. 6–8 | 112 |
| 6.1–6 | 118, 120 n., 129 |
| 6.2 | 97, 101, 118, 119, 122 |
| 6.3 | 129 n. |
| 6.5 | 101, 118 |
| 6.5 f. | 118, 122, 123 n. |
| 6.6 | 122 |
| 6.7 | 127, 128 |
| 6.7 ff. | 112 |
| 6.12 | 125 |
| 6.12 f. | 97, 128 |
| 6.13 | 77 n., 82, 83, 86, 88 |
| 6.14 | 118 |
| 6.14–29 | 73 |
| 6.20 | 117, 119 |
| 6.30 | 97, 112, 127 |
| 6.31 | 121 |
| 6.31 f. | 128 |
| 6.34 | 132 |
| 6.34–38 | 89 |
| 6.34–44 | 131 |
| 6.34–7.23 | 133 n. |
| 6.35 | 128 |
| 6.41 | 128 |
| 6.42–44 | 89 |
| 6.43 | 133 |
| 6.45 | 121, 128 |
| 6.49 | 118 |
| 6.49–52 | 117 |
| 6.50 | 97, 118, 121, 123 |
| 6.50 f. | 122 |
| 6.51 | 124 |
| 6.52 | 99, 118, 122, 124 |
| 7.1 | 120 |
| 7.1 ff. | 92, 106, 113, 130 |
| 7.1–14 | 124 |
| 7.2 | 128 |
| 7.2–5 | 132 |
| 7.3 f. | 112 |
| 7.4 | 132 |

| Bible Ref. Mark | Page |
|---|---|
| 7.5 f. | 121 |
| 7.5–15 | 92 |
| 7.5–23 | 92 |
| 7.6 | 105 |
| 7.6 f. | 106, 120 |
| 7.9–13 | 132 |
| 7.10 | 106 |
| 7.10–13 | 130 |
| 7.11 | 96 |
| 7.14 | 124 |
| 7.14–15 | 93, 120 |
| 7.17 | 124, 125, 128 |
| 7.17–23 | 93 |
| 7.18 | 99, 120, 124 |
| 7.19 | 124 |
| 7.21 f. | 132 |
| 7.24 ff | 130 |
| 7.24–30 | 112 |
| 7.25 | 83 |
| 7.25–30 | 132 |
| 7.26 | 77 n., 83 n., 86, 88 |
| 7.28 | 130, 132 |
| 7.29 | 83 n. |
| 7.30 | 83 n. |
| 7.32–37 | 125 |
| 7.33 | 120 n., 121 |
| 7.34 | 93 n., 98 n. |
| 7.35 | 88, 89 |
| 7.36 | 86 n., 97 |
| 7.37 | 119, 120, 125 |
| 8.1 | 128 |
| 8.1 ff. | 131 |
| 8.1–3 | 89 |
| 8.1–9 | 131 |
| 8.1–28 | 133 |
| 8.2 | 132 |
| 8.4 f. | 89 |
| 8.6 | 128 |
| 8.8 | 89, 133 |
| 8.10 | 127 |
| 8.11 | 93, 99 |
| 8.11–12 | 92 |
| 8.12 | 113 n. |
| 8.13 | 121 |
| 8.14 | 124 |
| 8.14–21 | 131, 133 |
| 8.15 | 99 |
| 8.16 | 124 |
| 8.17 | 99, 124 |
| 8.18 | 99, 124 n. |

| Bible Ref. Mark | Page |
|---|---|
| 8.19 f. | 113 |
| 8.19–21 | 89 |
| 8.21 | 99, 124 |
| 8.22 | 98 n. |
| 8.22–26 | 125 |
| 8.24 | 89 |
| 8.25 | 89 |
| 8.26 | 90, 130 |
| 8.27–30 | 93, 128 |
| 8.31 | 98, 99 |
| 8.31–33 | 93 |
| 8.32 | 100, 117, 128 |
| 8.32–9.1 | 99 |
| 8.33 | 93, 99, 100 |
| 8.34 | 128 |
| 8.34–37 | 98, 100, 122 |
| 8.38–9.1 | 100, 108, 113 n., 121, 127, 129 n. |
| 9.1 | 101, 108, 127 |
| 9.2 | 121, 128, 130 |
| 9.6 | 122 |
| 9.7 | 129 n. |
| 9.8 | 127 |
| 9.9 | 128 |
| 9.11 | 127 |
| 9.11–13 | 106 n. |
| 9.12 | 127 |
| 9.12 f. | 105 |
| 9.13 | 73, 106, 127 |
| 9.14 | 128 |
| 9.14 f. | 121 |
| 9.14 ff. | 93, 130 |
| 9.14–27 | 82 |
| 9.14–29 | 125 |
| 9.15 | 120 n., 122 |
| 9.17 | 83, 87, 121 |
| 9.18 | 77 n., 86, 87, 118, 128 |
| 9.19 | 113 n., 121, 122, 123 n. |
| 9.20 | 83 n., 86 |
| 9.22 | 87 |
| 9.23 | 121, 122 |
| 9.23 f. | 123 n. |
| 9.24 | 130 |
| 9.25 | 83 n., 84, 87, 98 n. |
| 9.26 | 84, 86 |
| 9.27 | 87 |
| 9.28 | 77 n., 86, 121, 128 |
| 9.30 | 101, 121 |
| 9.31 | 98, 99, 128 |
| 9.32 | 117, 122 |

| Bible Ref. Mark | Page |
|---|---|
| 9.33–35 | 128 |
| 9.33–47 | 100 |
| 9.33–50 | 99 |
| 9.33–10.31 | 98 |
| 9.35 | 132 |
| 9.38 | 77 n., 82, 83 n., 86, 99, 123, 128 |
| 9.38–40 | 86, 93 |
| 9.39 | 101 |
| 9.41 | 123 |
| 9.41 f. | 128, 132 |
| 9.42–50 | 100 |
| 9.43 | 103 n., 108 n. |
| 9.43–47 | 108 n. |
| 9.45 | 103 n., 108 n. |
| 9.47 | 108 n. |
| 10.1 | 101, 127 |
| 10.2 | 93, 97 |
| 10.2 ff. | 106 |
| 10.2–9 | 92 |
| 10.2–12 | 92, 132 |
| 10.5 | 96, 99, 124 |
| 10.6 | 96, 130 |
| 10.6 f. | 96 |
| 10.7 f. | 106 |
| 10.10 | 128 |
| 10.13 | 128 |
| 10.13–16 | 93 |
| 10.17 | 127, 129 |
| 10.17–22 | 93 |
| 10.18 | 132 |
| 10.19 | 106 |
| 10.21 | 123, 127, 129 |
| 10.23 | 97, 127, 128 |
| 10.23–26 | 129 |
| 10.24 | 117, 122 |
| 10.25 | 97 |
| 10.26 | 117, 122 |
| 10.28 | 123, 129 |
| 10.28–31 | 127 |
| 10.29 | 103 n., 129 |
| 10.30 | 103, 108 n., 127, 129 |
| 10.32 | 116 n., 117, 120, 123, 128 |
| 10.33 | 99, 120, 124, 128 |
| 10.33 f. | 98 |
| 10.35 | 117, 130 n. |
| 10.35 ff. | 100 |
| 10.35–44 | 100 |
| 10.35–45 | 93, 98, 99, 130 |

| Bible Ref. Mark | Page |
|---|---|
| 10.37 | 117 |
| 10.38 f. | 74 n., 93, 106 |
| 10.41 | 100, 117 |
| 10.42 | 100, 117 |
| 10.42–45 | 113 |
| 10.45 | 85 n., 100, 112 n., 127, 131, 132 |
| 10.46 | 101, 128 |
| 10.46–52 | 125 |
| 10.49 | 123 |
| 10.52 | 122, 123 |
| 11.1 | 120, 128 |
| 11.9 | 127 |
| 11.10 | 106 |
| 11.11 | 120, 127, 128 |
| 11.12–14 | 97 |
| 11.14 | 128 |
| 11.15 | 120 |
| 11.15–19 | 97 |
| 11.17 | 96, 105, 112 n. |
| 11.18 | 117, 118, 119 |
| 11.20–24 | 97 |
| 11.22 | 122, 123 |
| 11.22–24 | 123 |
| 11.23 f. | 97, 123 |
| 11.25 | 125, 129 n. |
| 11.27 | 92, 120 |
| 11.28 f. | 101 |
| 11.30 | 80 n. |
| 11.31 | 123 |
| 11.32 | 73, 117, 118 |
| 11.33 | 101 |
| 12.1 | 124 |
| 12.1–11 | 114 |
| 12.2–5 | 106 |
| 12.6 | 129 n. |
| 12.7 | 114 |
| 12.9 | 112, 114 |
| 12.10 | 105 |
| 12.12 | 117, 118, 124 |
| 12.13 f. | 85 |
| 12.13–17 | 92, 96 |
| 12.15 | 93, 99 |
| 12.17 | 118 |
| 12.18–27 | 92 |
| 12.23 | 125 |
| 12.24 | 101 |
| 12.25 | 103 n., 107, 108 n., 129, 130 |
| 12.26 | 106 |

| Bible Ref. | Page |
|---|---|
| *Mark* | |
| 12.29–33 | 106, 121 |
| 12.34 | 97, 118 |
| 12.36 | 105 |
| 12.37 | 119 |
| 12.38–40 | 132 |
| 12.39 | 120 |
| 12.47 | 106 |
| ch. 13 | 98 |
| 13.1–2 | 93 |
| 13.2 | 120 |
| 13.3 | 128, 130 |
| 13.5 | 109 |
| 13.5 f. | 111 |
| 13.3–13 | 98 |
| 13.6 | 127 |
| 13.7 | 110, 111, 121 |
| 13.8 | 110 |
| 13.9 | 109, 111, 113, 120 |
| 13.9 ff. | 110 |
| 13.10 | 110, 111 n., 112 n. |
| 13.11 | 77 n., 98, 111 |
| 13.12 | 129 |
| 13.14 | 110, 120 |
| 13.14–20 | 110 n. |
| 13.14–27 | 98 |
| 13.21 | 110, 123 |
| 13.21 f. | 111 |
| 13.23 | 109 |
| 13.24 | 110 |
| 13.26 | 100, 108, 110, 127 |
| 13.27 | 108, 110, 112 n. |
| 13.28 | 124 |
| 13.28–37 | 98 |
| 13.29 | 124 |
| 13.30 | 113 n. |
| 13.31 | 108 n. |
| 13.32 | 108, 129 n. |
| 13.33 | 108, 109 |
| 13.34 | 109 |
| 13.35 | 109 |
| 13.35 f. | 127 |
| 13.37 | 109 |
| 14.2 | 121 |
| 14.3–9 | 93, 128 |
| 14.9 | 112 n. |
| 14.14 | 128 |
| 14.17 | 127, 128 |
| 14.20 | 128 |
| 14.22–24 | 131 |
| 14.22–25 | 130 |
| 14.24 | 112 n., 131, 132 |

| Bible Ref. | Page |
|---|---|
| *Mark* | |
| 14.25 | 131 |
| 14.28 | 104 |
| 14.33 | 118, 128, 130 |
| 14.34 ff. | 131 |
| 14.36 | 101, 118, 129 n. |
| 14.38 | 93, 99, 100, 118 |
| 14.39 | 101 |
| 14.41 f. | 101 |
| 14.43 | 128 |
| 14.49 | 105 |
| 14.50 | 100, 118 |
| 14.61 | 129 n. |
| 14.61 f. | 101 |
| 14.62 | 101, 127 |
| 14.66–72 | 100 |
| 14.67 | 127, 128 |
| 15.2 | 101 |
| 15.5 | 101, 119 |
| 15.23 | 101 |
| 15.30–32 | 101 |
| 15.32 | 123 |
| 15.36 | 127 |
| 15.39 | 118, 129 n. |
| 15.41 | 120, 123, 127, 132 |
| 15.43 | 118 |
| 15.44 | 119 |
| 16.6 | 121 |
| 16.7 | 104, 105, 128 |
| 16.8 | 105, 115, 117 |
| *Luke* | |
| 1.2 | 69 |
| 1.17 | 77 n. |
| 3.19 f. | 71 n. |
| 3.20 f. | 70 f. |
| 3.22 | 69 |
| 4.14 | 77 n. |
| 4.21 | 69 |
| 6.4 | 131 n. |
| 10.18 | 80 n. |
| 13.16 | 79 n., 88 n. |
| 18.12 | 131 n. |
| 21.34–36 | 111 n. |
| 23.4 | 113 n. |
| 23.5 | 69, 70 |
| 22.20 | 113 n. |
| 23.22 | 113 n. |
| 23.25 | 113 n. |
| 24.47 | 70 n. |
| *John* | |
| 1.1 | 69 |
| 1.5–11 | 120 |